Florence

the City
the Monuments
the Museums
the Medici

I Fratellini Via Cimatori
Perché no! ice cream
via Tavolini
Vernazzano via Tavolini

12 Florentine Itineraries

(*)panoramic view
Museums . . . in italics

Livorno
www.sillabe.it
info@sillabe.it

Managing Editor: *Maddalena Paola Winspeare*
Texts: *Ethel Santacroce*
Opificio delle Pietre Dure and Medici
Biographies: *Monica Guarraccino*
Graphic Design: *Laura Belforte*
Editing: *Giulia Bastianelli*
Translation: *Emily Ligniti*

Photo Credits: *Archivio Sillabe: Foto R. Bardazzi, P. Nannoni, N. Orsi Battaglini, Rabatti & Domingie, G. Valsecchi, S. Zinelli*

ISBN 88-8347-309-4

A BIT of HISTORY

Perspective map known as "della Catena," *"Firenze com'era" Museum*

Piazza della Repubblica, Column of Abundance, *on the site of the ancient Roman forum*

Castagna Tower

Tabernacle of S. Maria della Tromba (*Palazzo dell'Arte della Lana*)

Ruins of the 14th-century walls with the Mascherino Tower

Though its origins are Etruscan, Florence was actually founded in 59 B.C. by the Romans who built an encampment along the Arno River called *Florentia.*

You can still make out the ancient *cardus* and *decumanus* in Piazza della Repubblica near the Column of Abundance between Via Roma-Via Calimala (*cardus maximus*) and Strozzi-Via del Corso (*decumanus maximus*). Even the city's partition into 4 sections dates back to Roman times.

During the barbarian invasions, Florence was besieged by the Ostrogoths (405), though its towering walls kept the invaders from entering the city. Then came the Byzantines (535) and finally the Goths, who captured Florence in 541.

During the Carolingians (8th cent.), the city became part of the Holy Roman Empire. It was later controlled by Countess Matilde of Canossa. In 1115, when the Countess died, Florence was able to transform itself into an independent commune governed by influential rich merchants, powerful members of the clergy, and prominent noble families.

The city was often divided between two factions: the Guelphs (loyal to the Pope) and the Ghibellines (supporters of the Emperor). These two factions repeatedly

clashed (the Ghibelline victory at Montaperti in 1260 is emblematic).
In 1289, the Guelphs were able to defeat Arezzo at Campaldino. This decisive battle resulted in Florence's complete domination over the other cities in Tuscany.
Despite the mutually destructive rivalry between these two factions, Florence began its climb to the top thanks to its famous wool and silk trade. In 1252, the city minted its own gold coins, called *Florins*, with the image of the iris (the city's flower-symbol) on one side and *St. John the Baptist* (Florence's patron saint whose feast day is still celebrated on June 24) on the other.
As the economy thrived, the 7 Major Guilds, artisan corporations made up of bankers, wealthy merchants, and financiers of European rulers, began governing the city.
In 1293, the new nobility who had become rich as merchants obtained the "Ordinance of Justice" by excluding the prominent old aristocracy families from ruling the city.
But with the Hundred Years War, the crisis of Florentine banks (they had financed the insolvent King of England, Edward III), and the catastrophic outbreak of the Black Death in 1348, the lower classes slowly grew intolerant and revolted against those who belonged to the Major Guilds in the famous "Ciompi" uprising. Those who manufactured wool were able to form a Guild and take part in the government. But shortly afterwards, the new Guilds were abolished and power was reclaimed by a few prominent families. The city split in two: those who were loyal to the old oligarchy, which revolved around the Albizi family, and those of more modest means—devotees of the Medici family, who came from the Mugello area and were rich bankers.
The *Florentine Republic* gained access to the sea by capturing Pisa and Livorno. Cosimo the Elder de' Medici made the city

into a Signoria in 1434, thereby paving the way for centuries of cultural and political splendor. Cosimo ruled from his palazzo on Via Larga (Palazzo Medici-Riccardi), whereas Palazzo Vecchio, the seat of the magistracy, lost more and more importance.
It was his grandson, Lorenzo the Magnificent, who consolidated, during the second-half of the 15th century, Medici supremacy and prestige thanks to his brilliant political strategy in which he forged alliances with powerful families in Naples and Milan. However, his son Piero was exiled because he proved incapable of keeping the French troops of Charles VIII out of Florence (1494). The Florentines reacted to this invasion with uprisings, exhorted by the preaching of friar Savonarola (excommunicated for heresy and burned at the stake in Piazza della Signoria). The *Republic* was re-established until 1512, which was when the Magnificent's sons returned to the city: Giovanni (who became Pope Leo X) and Giuliano, though both were later forced to seek refuge in Rome (1527). Florence then reinstated the Republic and appointed the Duke of Urbino as the city's Captain. In the meantime, the Medici were gaining more and more power in Rome, and even Giuliano de' Medici's illegitimate son, Giulio, was elected Pope Clement VII. After the Sack of Rome in 1527, this new pope forged an alliance with Emperor Charles V to besiege Florence (1530). The city surrendered in 1532. Once the Medici returned, Florence was transformed into a Duchy with Alessandro I, and then into a *Grand Duchy* with Cosimo I (1569), the son of Giovanni of the Black Bands, who was able to subjugate Siena. With him and his successors, Francesco I and Ferdinando I, many important constructions were built and the city flourished both culturally and economically. This magnificence lasted until 1737 when the last representative of the family, Gian Gastone, died without an heir. As a result,

Tuscany was assigned to Francesco Stefano of Lorraine, the husband of Maria Teresa, the Empress of Austria. Thus began a long period of close ties with the Hapsburg-Lorraines, and the city was ruled by a Regency Council until 1765. In that year, Grand Duke Pietro Leopoldo, Maria Teresa's second child, arrived in Florence and implemented important administrative, financial, and agricultural reforms. The French Revolution brought Tuscany under French control during the reign of Elisa Baciocchi, Napoleon's sister. However, the Lorraines reclaimed power with Ferdinando III until 1860, the year in which the Grand Duchy was annexed to the Kingdom of Italy of King Vittorio Emanuele II of Savoy. As Italy's new capital (1865-1870), Florence underwent drastic urban changes: streets and palazzos were built at the expense of important historical landmarks, such as the ancient walls, and large industries were established. During World War II, Florence was plagued by clashes between partisans and German troops; it was heavily bombed and centuries-old sections were completely destroyed. However, Ponte Vecchio was spared. In fact, the bridge even survived the 1966 flooding of the Arno, and today it has become a symbol of the city.

B. Poccetti and helpers, Map of Livorno, *Palazzo Pitti, Room of Bona*

Florentine painter, Piazza della Signoria with the Martyrdom of Savonarola, *Museum of S. Marco*

O. Vannini, Lorenzo among the Artists, *detail*, *Palazzo Pitti, Museo degli Argenti*

1. DUOMO and ORSANMICHELE

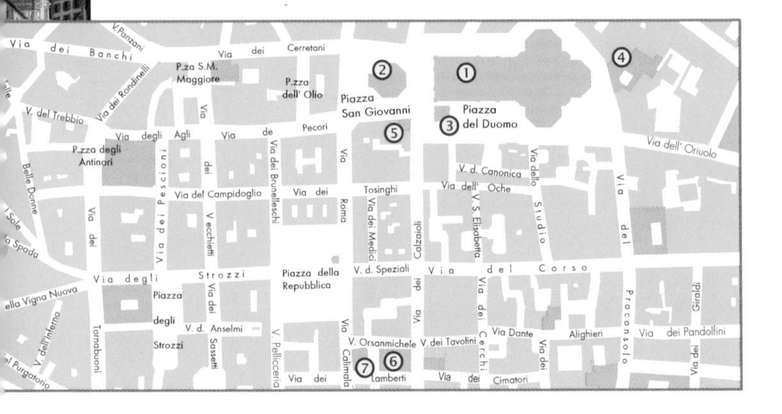

Piazza del Duomo and Piazza di S. Giovanni
As the city's religious center, you'll find 3 of Florence's most important monuments on these 2 connecting squares: the Duomo, Giotto's Bell Tower, and the Baptistery.

❶ **Basilica of S. Maria del Fiore or Duomo** (hours: 10 am-5 pm)
The first thing that catches your eye is the size of this church. It's 153 meters long, 38 meters wide at the nave, and 90 meters at the transept. In fact, it can hold 30,000 people. This is indeed one of the largest cathedrals in the world!
The present-day basilica was built upon a pre-existing church dedicated to S. Reparata (4th-5th cent.). During the 1966 excavations, the ruins of this church were found in the front part of the nave (you can visit these from the crypt).
The church was started in 1296 by the architect **A. di Cambio**,

who began constructing the Palazzo della Signoria at the same time. The basilica took about 140 years to complete (it was consecrated in 1436 by Pope Eugene IV), and famous architects like **Giotto** (1334-1337 ca.), **A. Pisano**, **F. Talenti**, and **L. Ghini** took turns supervising the work. The way the church looks today dates back to 1887 when the neo-Gothic marble façade was finally completed by the architect **E. De Fabris**.
For the FAÇADE, De Fabris was inspired by a drawing of A. di Cambio based upon the glorification of the Madonna. In fact, in the section above the main doors you'll see a *Gallery of the Apostles* with a central aedicule representing the *Virgin and Child.*
In the tympanum are the bas-relief of the *Eternal Father* and busts of celebrated artists. In the tabernacles of the pilasters, you'll find images of clergy members who played an important role in building this cathedral. The bronze doors, portraying the *Stories of Mary*, are by A. Passaglia and G. Cassioli (late 19th cent.).
The INTERIOR, with its Gothic layout, is in the form of a Latin cross with 3 naves divided by pillars topped with arches. The multicolored marble floor is attributed to **B. d'Agnolo**.
In the area in front of the CHAPEL OF THE CROSS in the left tribune, there's a meridian that was used to study astronomy by many scholars of the age.
The INTERIOR FAÇADE has 3 round stained glass windows designed by Ghiberti. The *clock* with prophet heads by **P. Uccello** is quite curious (1443). Below you'll see a lunette with a *Crowned Mary* by **G. Gaddi** and the *Tomb of Bishop Antonino d'Orso* (1321).
In the RIGHT NAVE, observe the *bust of Filippo Brunelleschi* (1446) by **Buggiano**, the *bust of Giotto* (1490) by **B. da Maiano**, and the splendid Gothic *stoup* (14th cent.).

The DOME INTERIOR was frescoed beginning in 1572 by **G. Vasari**, but F. Zuccari completed it in 1579 with scenes taken from the *Last Judgement*.
At the end of the 2 side naves you'll see the door that allows you to climb up to the DOME. It's a long way up a narrow flight of steps (463), but your efforts will be rewarded with the breath-taking view of the city.
The stained glass windows of the tambour were designed by Renaissance masters such as L. Ghiberti, P. Uccello, Donatello, and A. del Castagno.
At the CENTER OF THE OCTAGON you'll find the *marble chorus* and the *main altar* (1555), both by **B. Bandinelli** and **G. Bandini**; the wooden *crucifix* on the altar is by **B. da Maiano** (1497).
In the CENTRAL TRIBUNE, under the altar you'll see the bronze urn, made by L. Ghiberti (1430-1440), that contains the relics of St.

Zenobius, Florence bishop.
The 3 tribunes around the transept are separated by 2 sacristies: the OLD SACRISTY (or the Sacristy of Canons) and the NEW SACRISTY (or the Sacristy of Masses). The 2 entrances are topped with glazed terracotta lunettes by **L. della Robbia** (1444 ca.) and respectively portray the *Ascension* and the *Resurrection.* In the LEFT NAVE (bay IV), observe the painting by **D. di Michelino** depicting *Dante with the City of Florence, Hell, Purgatory, and Paradise* (1465).
As you head towards the exit, you'll come across 2 other monochrome frescoes dedicated to 2 illustrious leaders, *Giovanni Acuto*, by **P. Uccello** (1436), and *Niccolò da Tolentino*, by **A. del Castagno** (1456). You can also admire the bust of the organist *Antonio Squarcialupi* (1490) by **B. da Maiano**.
More recent works in the cathedral include *Arnolfo di Cambio* by **U. Cambi** (1843) and *Emilio De Fabris* by **V. Consani** (1887). In the LEFT NAVE, there's also a lovely aedicule dedicated to St. Zenobius.

DOME (*PANORAMIC VIEW)
The famous dome by **F. Brunelleschi**, whose tomb can be found in the crypt, is approximately 115 meters in height and 45 meters in diameter. It occupies the great octagonal tambour between the transepts. It was begun in 1420 after Brunelleschi had won the competition announced 2 years earlier. His project was innovatory and consisted in using a double-shelled self-supporting ribbed structure and a wall structure made up of bricks arranged in a herringbone pattern so as to provide greater compactness and solidity.
The work continued until 1436, the year in which Brunelleschi also began designing the lantern that would complete the cu-

Duomo:
G. Vasari and F. Zuccari, Last Judgement, *detail*
D. di Michelino, Dante with the City of Florence, Hell, Purgatory, and Paradise
Buggiano, Bust of Brunelleschi
P. Uccello, Monument to Giovanni Acuto
Sacristy of the Masses

pola. However, it was **Verrocchio**, in 1471, who finished the lantern by placing the gilt bronze sphere on top.

Venetian mosaicists, Mosaics on the Baptistery vault, detail

Museum of the Opera di S. Maria del Fiore:

A. di Cambio, Madonna with Blessing Child

Michelangelo, Pietà

Donatello, Penitent Magdalene

❷ Baptistery

A fine example of 11th-century Romanesque architecture, its layout is octagonal and it has a diameter of 26 meters (ca.). Its roof is pyramid-shaped and topped by a lantern with columns; it is also covered in white and green marble. It was the city's cathedral until 1128 and is dedicated to St. John the Baptist. Many illustrious men of Florence, including Dante, were baptized here. The INTERIOR consists in a single room embellished with marble and Byzantine-style mosaics on the vault. The images represent the *Heavenly Hierarchies*, *Stories of the Genesis*, *Stories of Mary and Jesus*, *Stories of St. John the Baptist*, and the *Last Judgement*.
The marble baptismal font (1371) attributed to the Pisan school is rather interesting. The *Tomb of the anti-Pope John XXIII* by **Donatello** and **Michelozzo** is also lovely. You'll be able to see the remains (walls and mosaic floor) of a Roman house through a grid on the floor.
The Baptistery has 3 BRONZE DOORS: the one to the south is by **A. Pisano** (1336) and is divided into 28 tiles with *Stories of St. John the Baptist* and the *Cardinal and Theological Virtues*. The other doors (1403-1452) are both by **Ghiberti**. The one on the north side, also called the "Cross Door," depicts 20 scenes from the *New Testament* and 8 tiles with the *Fathers of the Church* and the *Evangelists*.
Michelangelo defined the east door as the *Gate of Heaven*. Ghiberti used perspective for the 10 gilt bronze tiles obtained with the "schiacciato" technique (flattened relief). The bas-reliefs depict *Stories from the Old Testament* enclosed

in a frame with 24 niches representing biblical figures and 24 heads of artists including Ghiberti's own self-portrait (he is bald and is the fourth from the top on the right side of the left panel).

❸ GIOTTO'S BELL TOWER

To the right of the cathedral you'll find the Bell Tower (also called "Giotto's Bell Tower"). Giotto began working on this splendid structure in 1334. With its square-shaped base, it is over 84 meters in height. You can access it from the rear exit of the cathedral. It's another long flight up (414 steps), but the wonderful *VIEW OF THE CITY from on top is well worth it. Giotto was able to finish the first part of the foundations with hexagonal tiles. However, the work was completed by **F. Talenti** in 1359. The iconography of the lower section illustrates scenes of *Planets*, *Virtues*, *Human Activities*, *Liberal Arts*, *Sacraments*..

❹ MUSEUM OF THE OPERA DI S. MARIA DEL FIORE (Piazza del Duomo, 9)

Inaugurated in 1891, it gathers sculptures, drawings, and vestments that were once located in the Baptistery, the Duomo, and the Bell Tower.
In the ROOM OF THE DUOMO'S ANCIENT FAÇADE, works gathered from the 1587 façade demolition are found here. These include works by **A. di Cambio**, **Donatello**, and **N. di Banco**.
The 2 BRUNELLESCHI ROOMS display wooden models of the dome, the artist's funerary mask, and tools used while building the cupola. In the display cases, you'll also see *Illuminated Antiphonaries* (1525), objects in gold, and liturgical vestments.
On the floor above you'll find **Michelangelo**'s *Pietà* (1553), a work the artist intended for his own funerary chapel in Rome. It was brought here in 1980. In the ROOM OF THE CHOIR, you can admire

Donatello, Choir
Church of Orsanmichele:
Donatello and Verrocchio, Tabernacle with Doubting Thomas
Orcagna and B. Daddi, Tabernacle with the Madonna of the Graces

those by **L. della Robbia** and **Donatello** (he is also the artist of the *Penitent Magdalene*, a wooden statue, 1455). Next come the ROOM OF THE TILES OF GIOTTO'S BELL TOWER and the ALTAR ROOM where Ghiberti's tiles, once located on the Gate of Heaven, are displayed.

❺ LOGGIA DEL BIGALLO (corner between Piazza Duomo and Via Calzaiuoli)
Of late Gothic style, this loggia was commissioned by the Compagnia della Misericordia to **A. Arnoldi**. Work was started in the mid-1300s. It was initially used as the Confraternity headquarters. Today, the **BIGALLO MUSEUM** is located here; it gathers works commissioned by the Bigallo Captains over the centuries (1300s-1700s), including the lovely *Madonna of Mercy* (1342). From here you'll see the most ancient section of Florence. The outside is covered in marble with reliefs representing biblical figures.

❻ CHURCH OF ORSANMICHELE (access from Via Arte della Lana)
Located in front of the Church of S. Carlo, its name derives from the ancient oratory of S. Michele in Orto. This was replaced in 1290 by **A. di Cambio** to host the grain loggia-market. In 1380, the building became

a church and the outside arcades were closed off. Tabernacles were then made to contain the bronze and marble statues of the patron saints of the various Guilds, commissioned to some of the city's most prominent artists (15th-17th cent.).
Observe the splendid statues of *St. Matthew*, *St. Stephen*, and *St. John the Baptist* by **L. Ghiberti**; *St. George* (the original is found in the Bargello), *St. Peter*, and *St. Mark* by **Donatello**; *St. Lucy* by **Giambologna**; *St. Thomas* by **Verrocchio**; *Four Crowned Saints* by **N. di Banco**. Some of these statues are copies of the originals you can admire in the museum spaces recently opened to the public on the floors above the church.
The INTERIOR is rectangular, divided into 2 naves supported by pillars frescoed in the 1300s with images of the patron saints of the Minor Guilds and scenes from the Old and New Testaments.
At the end of the RIGHT NAVE there's the splendid *Tabernacle* by **A. Orcagna** (1355-1359); it is shaped like a baldachin and is embellished with gold and colored marble. At the center of the altar you'll see the altarpiece representing the *Madonna of the Graces* by **B. Daddi** (1347). Around the base there are scenes of the life and virtues of Mary, whereas on the back you'll find the artist's signature.
You'll find, on the north side, traces of when this place was used as a grain market: a weight and an outfall.

❼ **PALAZZO DELL'ARTE DELLA LANA** (1308)
Adjacent to Orsanmichele (actually, it's connected by a raised corridor), it was the palazzo of the richest Major Guilds. It looks like a house-tower and today the offices of the Società Dantesca are located here, as can be seen by a fresco on the outside depicting the poet Dante.

2. PIAZZA della SIGNORIA and the UFFIZI

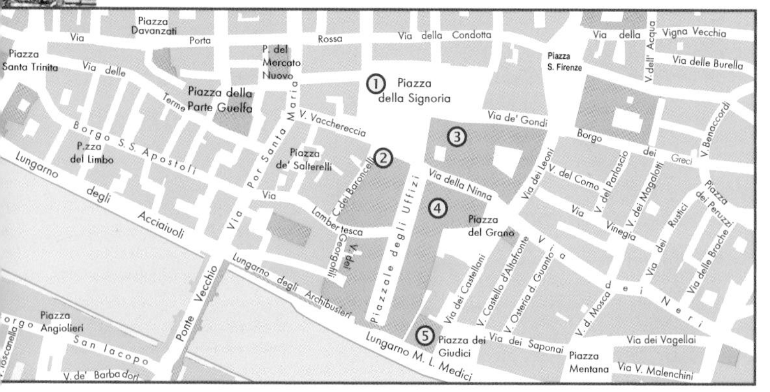

❶ Piazza della Signoria

This square is still considered the political center of the city. On the left you'll find the *Equestrian Monument of Cosimo I* (1594) by the Flemish artist **Giambologna**; there's also a marble fountain (1575) by **B. Ammannati** portraying *Neptune* (also called "il Biancone") on a chariot drawn by sea horses with bronze satyrs and nymphs. A round granite plaque, located in front of the fountain, commemorates the site where the preacher Savonarola was burned at the stake in 1498. On the steps leading to Palazzo Vecchio you can admire, from left to right: the *Marzocco*, or a lion (in fact, a few real ones were kept at the back of the palace!). These animals were also one of the city's symbols. The original statue (1438) is by **Donatello** and can be found at the Bargello Museum. Next you'll find a recent bronze copy of *Judith and Holofernes* (1460), also by Donatello (the original is kept in the Fleur-de-Lis Hall inside the

palazzo). There's also a marble copy of **Michelangelo**'s *David* (the original is on display at the Accademia Gallery). And finally, there's *Hercules and Cacus* by **B. Bandinelli** (1534).

❷ Loggia dei Lanzi

Also known as the "Loggia della Signoria," it was intended as a meeting point for public assemblies and ceremonies during the Signoria. The loggia was built by B. di Cione and S. Talenti between 1376 and 1382 and is based upon a drawing by A. Orcagna. After the fall of the Florentine Republic, the "Lanzichenecchi" (lansquenets) of Duke Alessandro I de' Medici occupied the loggia (that's how it got its derogatory name "dei Lanzi"). Cosimo I transformed the loggia's function from political to artistic and allowed it to become a place for artists and sculptors.
Late-Gothic in style, the loggia is decorated with lobed tiles with emblems of the Florentine Republic symbolizing the *theological and cardinal Virtues*. On the right in the first row, you'll find the lovely marble *Rape of the Sabines* (1583) and *Hercules and the Centaur* (1599), both by **Giambologna**. Next there's a Hellenic copy of *Menelaus Holding the Dead Body of Patroclus*, whereas the *Rape of Polissena* by **P. Fedi** is more recent (1866).
Under the left arch you'll see the splendid bronze *Perseus* (1554) by **B. Cellini** as he displays Medusa's slain head. The hero's bandoleer bears the artist's name and date. You'll also see 6 Roman statues of women against the back wall.

❸ Palazzo Vecchio

The **Palazzo dei Priori** (also known as Palazzo "Vecchio" or Palazzo della "Signoria"), with its parallelepiped-shape, is truly a splendid building.

Conceived in 1293 as a civil monument intended to host the Priors, **A. di Cambio** began working on the palace in 1299. In the 15th century, it passed to the Signoria, and was called "Vecchio" (old) when Cosimo I decided to move his residence from here to Palazzo Pitti (1565). Between 1865 and 1870 the Italian Parliament was located here when Florence was the nation's capital. Since 1872, the Municipality's administrative offices are found here.
The palace resembles a fortified structure with a majestic bell tower (1310) 94 meters high. Covered in rustic ashlar-work in *pietra forte*, it is divided into 3 levels, 2 of which have mullioned windows. On the top section you'll see a row of arches adorned with the 9 emblems of the Florentine Republic. There's also a landing shielded by Guelph merlons. The palazzo was enlarged over the years (starting in 1453). Michelozzo, Vasari (1558), and B. Buontalenti (1588) all worked on the palace. Vasari is credited with the decorations in the FIRST COURTYARD with grotesque art and frescoes with views of cities of the Hapsburg Empire (1565) that were executed on the occasion of the wedding festivities of Francesco I de' Medici and Giovanna of Austria. At the center you'll find the *Putto with Dolphin* fountain (1476) by **Verrocchio**. You should then reach the COURTYARD OF CUSTOMS where you'll see a weather-vane with a lion and a lily, originally located on the top of the tower.
HALL OF THE FIVE HUNDRED - Take either grand staircase (made by Vasari). You'll reach the celebrated "Salone dei Cinquecento" designed by **Cronaca** in 1495. This room (53 meters long and 22 meters wide) was intended to meet the needs of the Republican government by hosting the General Council.
In 1563, it became a reception hall under Cosimo I, who had it frescoed by Vasari. The artist sought the help of various collaborators to decorate the walls and ceiling with scenes depicting the

Palazzo Vecchio: *first courtyard*
Hall of the Five Hundred
Francesco I's Studiolo

Apotheosis of Cosimo I and with allegories of the city's sections, of the provinces subjugated by the Grand Duke, of stories about Florence, of the episodes of war against Pisa and Siena.

HEARING HALL (north wall) - Located in a raised position with respect to the rest of the hall, it was intended for the Grand Duke's throne. In the niches, you'll see marble statues including those by **Bandinelli**: from the left *Cosimo I*, then *Giovanni of the Black Bands*, *Leo X*, and *Alessandro de' Medici*. On the wall opposite the entrance you'll find the *Genius of Victory* (1534) by **Michelangelo**, a work that was initially intended for the tomb of Pope Julius II.

STUDIOLO OF FRANCESCO I (door to the left of the entrance) - Decorated by Vasari (1572) and pupils, this was dedicated to Francesco's studies in science. The walls hide cabinets where the Prince jealously kept his collections and are adorned with the allegorical figures of *Prometheus*, the *Four Elements*, and man's activities. At the corners of the vault you'll see various human states of mind. In the lunette tondos, you'll find the portraits of *Eleanor of Toledo* and *Cosimo I* by **Bronzino**. The small statues in the niches represent mythological divinities.

The cabinets hide the *Tesoretto* (desk) Cosimo I commissioned in 1559 to contain his treasures (this was also decorated by Vasari with the symbols of the 4 Evangelists).

APARTMENTS OF LEO X (access from the Hall of the Five Hundred) - Composed of 6 rooms with Vasarian paintings (1562) that celebrate the Medici family.

The HALL dedicated to Leo X is frescoed with episodes from the life of Cardinal Giovanni, Lorenzo de' Medici's son who became pope in 1513, and marble busts portraying members of the Medici family. The other rooms cannot be visited in that they are administrative offices; these include the HALL OF CLEMENT VII (with the fresco

Siege of Florence of 1529-1530), the HALL OF GIOVANNI OF THE BLACK BANDS, the HALL OF COSIMO I, the HALL OF LORENZO THE MAGNIFICENT, and the HALL OF COSIMO THE ELDER. Each of these rooms is decorated with portraits and scenes from the life of the person it is dedicated to.

APARTMENTS OF THE ELEMENTS (access from the Hall of Leo X) - Composed of 5 rooms designed by G.B. del Tasso (1550) and decorated by Vasari and his assistants. The first room, called the HALL OF ELEMENTS, is embellished with scenes that refer to the 4 primary elements, whereas the marble fireplace was designed by Ammannati. There's a spectacular view of the city from the LOGGIATO OF SATURN. (*PANORAMIC VIEW)

There are also the HALL OF HERCULES (with paintings of the *Labors of Hercules* and an ebony cabinet with semi-precious stones), the HALL OF JOVE (with 16th-century Florentine tapestries and the original *Putto with Dolphin* statue by Verrocchio), and the HALL OF CERES (with 16th-century tapestries and paintings).

APARTMENTS OF ELEANOR OF TOLEDO (access from the landing that faces the Hall of the Five Hundred) - The ceiling of the GREEN HALL is decorated with grotesque art by **R. del Ghirlandaio**. Next you'll see the chapel with frescoes by **Bronzino**, who also painted the lovely altarpiece (1540-1545). Other rooms include the HALL OF THE SABINES, the HALL OF ESTHER (with a 15th-century marble lavabo and Florentine tapestries), the HALL OF PENELOPE, and the GUALDRADA ROOM (a bedroom dedicated to marital fidelity and decorated with scenes of games and festivities by the Flemish artist Jan Van der Straet).

Chapel of Eleanor
Hearing Hall
Fleurs-de-Lis Hall

CHAPEL OF THE PRIORS OR OF THE SIGNORIA - This chapel was built by **B. d'Agnolo** (1514) and was decorated by Ghirlandaio with biblical scenes.

HEARING HALL (from the marble doorway in the Chapel) - Created by **B. da Maiano**, here you can admire the gilded ceiling with octagonal coffers bearing the emblem of the Florentine people (by **G. da Maiano**, 1478).
FLEUR-DE-LIS HALL - This room stands out for its magnificent marble entrance by **G.** and **B. da Maiano** (1481) with inlaid panels representing Dante and Petrarch. The wood ceiling is decorated with gold lilies set against a sky-blue background (the lily was the symbol of the Anjou family). You'll also find here the original *Judith and Holofernes* (1460 ca.), **Donatello**'s masterpiece.
Other rooms include the GUARDAROBA (or storage room) or the HALL OF MAPS where the Medici stored their precious objects. If you head to the MEZZANINE, you'll reach the 3 rooms that host the *Loeser Collection* (seasonal opening), donated in 1928 to the Municipality by the American art critic Charles Loeser. It gathers Tuscan school paintings and sculptures (14th-16th cent.).

❹ THE UFFIZI
Right next to Palazzo Vecchio you'll find the Uffizi, commissioned to Vasari by Cosimo I de' Medici in 1560; he wanted to reunite the 13 city magistracies in a single location. Vasari decided to make the most of the area that extends towards the Arno. He demolished the buildings, including the Romanesque Church of S. Pier Scheraggio, that were there. The project consisted in 2 long, Doric-style porticos that went from Palazzo Vecchio to the Loggia della Signoria, joined by a splendid loggia in the section facing the Arno. (*PANORAMIC VIEW)
On the back arch you'll find the *Statue of Cosimo I* (1585) by **Giambologna**, whereas in the niches against the pillars you'll see statues of prominent Tuscans.

Uffizi:
Gallery Corridor
A. del Castagno, Queen Tomiri
Leonardo, Woman's Head

The work was completed in 1580 by A. Parigi and B. Buontalenti, who followed the desire of Francesco I (Cosimo I's successor) to make the Uffizi into a Gallery. A Tribune was created (1584) where the Grand Duke placed his most prized treasures. The offices were moved to other locations and the Gallery of Greek and Roman statues began to take shape. His successors enriched the collection with other sculptures, mathematical instruments, and scientific rarities. In the 1600s, Vittoria della Rovere's dowry consisted in an impressive quantity of works of art including many paintings by Raphael, Titian, and Piero della Francesca. More works, especially paintings, arrived with Cardinal Leopoldo, Cosimo II, and Pietro Leopoldo. The "Family Pact" (1737) between Anna Maria Luisa, the last Medici, and the Lorraine family was decisive in that she bound the entire Medici collection to the city of Florence with the obligation of making it accessible to the public.

ENTRANCE AND VESTIBULE - On the ground floor you'll see the remains of the Church of S. Pier Scheraggio and the frescoes of *Illustrious Men* (mid-1400s) by **A. del Castagno** (try to identify Dante, Petrarch, and Boccaccio). On the right wall you'll see the painting of **C. Cagli**, the *Battle of*

St. Martin (1936). On the left, the *Annunciation* (1481) by **Botticelli**.

GABINETTO DEI DISEGNI E DELLE STAMPE - Located on the floor above, this room contains drawings and prints by Italian and foreign artists (15th-20th cent.). There are also originals by Leonardo, Raphael, and Michelangelo. Continue on to the next floor. You'll reach the corridors with ceilings that are adorned with grotesque art by 16th-century Florentine masters.

ROOM 1 - Gathers classical sculptures, mostly Roman. A copy of the *Doryphorus* by Polyclitus and the *Athlete* stand out.

ROOM 2 THE DUECENTO AND GIOTTO - This room resembles a medieval church. It displays lovely crucifixes and works by Tuscan school artists such as **Giotto** with his *Ognissanti Majesty* (1310 ca.) and the *Badia Polyptych* (1300 ca.); **Cimabue** with the *St. Trinita Majesty* (1280-1290 ca.); **D. di Buoninsegna** with his *Rucellai Madonna* (1285 ca.).

ROOM 3 THE SIENESE TRECENTO - Room dedicated to the pupils of Duccio and Giotto. On display are works by **S. Martini** (the splendid gold *Annunciation* triptych, 1333), **A. Lorenzetti** (*Presentation at the Temple*, 1342, and the *Stories of St. Nicholas of Bari*, 1330 ca.), **P. Lorenzetti** (*Altarpiece of the Blessed Humility*, 1340 ca., and the *Madonna and Child Enthroned with Angels*, 1340?).

ROOM 4 THE FLORENTINE TRECENTO - This room gathers Giotto school paintings. These include *St. Cecilia and Stories of her Life* (1304 ca.) attributed to the **Master of the S. Cecilia**; the *Madonna Enthroned with Angels and Saints* (1355) by **T. Gaddi**; the *Madonna with Child and St. Matthew and St. Nicholas* (1328) and the *Polyptych of St. Pancras* by **B. Daddi**. There are also works by **Nardo di Cione** (*Crucifixion*, 1350 ca.) and **Andrea di Cione**, also known as **Orcagna** (*Triptych of St. Matthew*). But the painting that is most similar to Giotto's style is the *Pi-*

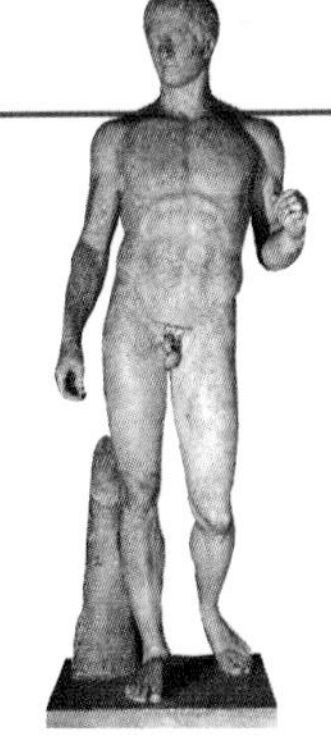

Doryphorus, *Roman copy*
Giotto, Madonna d'Ognissanti
S. Martini and L. Memmi, Annunciation
G. da Fabriano, Adoration of the Magi

P. Uccello, Battle of St. Romano
P. della Francesca, Diptych of the Dukes of Urbino
Masaccio and Masolino, St. Anna Metterza
Filippino Lippi, Adoration of the Magi
Filippo Lippi, Madonna and Child with Two Angels
Botticelli, The Return of Judith to Betulia

età (second-half 14th cent.*)* by **Giottino**.

ROOMS 5-6 INTERNATIONAL GOTHIC - Rooms dedicated to Italian painters of the late 14th and early 15th centuries (this period is known as Late Gothic or "flowery" Gothic for the abundance of decoration). Here you'll see the *Crucifixion* by **A. Gaddi**, the son of Taddeo; the *Madonna with Child* by **J. Bellini**; the *Adoration of the Magi* (1423) and the *Four Saints from the Quaratesi Polyptych* by **G. da Fabriano**; the *Crowning of the Virgin* (1414) and the *Adoration of the Magi* (1420 ca.) by **L. Monaco.**

ROOM 7 EARLY RENAISSANCE - On display are important works by Tuscan painters (early 1400s). You'll see paintings by **P. della Francesca** (his famous *Diptych of the Dukes of Urbino*, 1472 ca., portraits of Federico da Montefeltro and his wife Battista Sforza; on the back there's the Flemish-style allegory of the *Dukes in Triumph*); **P. Uccello** (*Battle of St. Romano*, undated, was painted for the apartments of Cosimo the Elder); **Masaccio** (*Madonna with Child*); **Masaccio** and **Masolino** (*St. Anne Metterza*, 1424 ca.). Masaccio-inspired works include those by **B. Angelico** (*Crowning of the Virgin*, 1435 ca., and the *Madonna with Child*). Another masterpiece is the *Altarpiece of St. Lucy de' Magnoli* (1445 ca.) by **Veneziano**.

ROOM 8 LIPPI - This room is dedicated to the Carmelite monk and his pupils. You'll find Lippi's *Novitiate Altarpiece* (1445 ca.), the *Pala Barbadori* predella, the splendid *Crowning of the Virgin* (1447), the 2 *Adoration of the Child*, and the lovely *Madonna with Child and Two Angels* (1465 ca.) that inspired Botticelli. His pupils include his son **Filippino Lippi** with the *Adoration of the Magi* (1496) and *St. Jerome*, and **A. Baldovinetti** with the *Annunciation* and the *Madonna with Child and Saints*.

ROOM 9 POLLAIOLO - Here you'll find works by the brothers **Antonio** and **Piero del Pollaiolo**. Look especially for the *Portrait of a Lady* (1475 ca.) and the *Labors of Hercules* (1475 ca.), both by Antonio. The *Portrait of Galeazzo Maria Sforza* (1471) and *Six Virtues* are by Piero and were intended to adorn the Tribunale di Mercatanzia. The *Fortress* was painted by Botticelli in 1470. Other works by this artist as a young man can also be found in this room and include the *Story of Judith* series (1472 ca.).

ROOMS 10-14 BOTTICELLI - These rooms are dedicated to this legendary master. Here you'll see many of his works (1445-1510) and others by artists from late 15th-century Tuscan and Flemish schools.

Look especially for *St. Augustine in his Study*, the *Madonna of the Rose Garden*, and the *Portrait of a Youth with a Medal* (1475 ca.). In the early 1480s, **Botticelli** dedicated himself to "mythologies," or moral allegories that include *Pallas and the Centaur*, but especially the splendid *Primavera* and the *Birth of Venus*. You can also admire the *Madonna of the Magnificat*, the *Madonna of the Pomegranate* (1487) with its inlaid frame, the *St. Barnabus Altarpiece* (1487 ca.), the *Madonna in Glory with Cherubs* (1470 ca.), and *Calumny* (1495 ca.).

In these same rooms, paintings by others can also be seen including the *Portinari*

Triptych (1478 ca.) by the Flemish artist **H. van der Goes** and an *Adoration of the Magi* by **D. Ghirlandaio.**

ROOM 15 LEONARDO - This room is dedicated to **Leonardo** and to Tuscan and Umbrian painters of the late 1400s.

The legendary artist is present with his *Annunciation* (done while still a young man in around 1472) and the unfinished *Adoration of the Magi* (1481), which he started working on before leaving for Milan. In the *Baptism of Christ* (1475 ca.) of **A. del Verrocchio**, you can see Leonardo's touch in the figure of the angel on the left and in the background. There are also the *Crucifixion with Mary Magdalene* by **L. Signorelli**, the *Crucifixion with Saints* by **Perugino**, the *Adoration of the Shepherds* by **L. di Credi**, and the *Incarnation of Christ* (1505 ca.) by **P. di Cosimo**.

Rooms 16 to 24 constitute the museum's oldest corpus of works.

ROOM 16 MAP ROOM - The name of this room derives from the 3

geographical maps of Tuscany, frescoed in 1589 by **S. Buonsignori**. On the ceiling you'll also see 9 paintings by **J. Zucchi**.

ROOM 17 THE HERMAPHRODITE - Here you'll find the marble statue, a Roman copy, of the *Sleeping Hermaphrodite*.

ROOM 18 TRIBUNA - Created by Buontalenti, this octagon-shaped tribune was decorated by Poccetti and intended to gather the Medici family's most prized treasures. You can admire copies of classical statues like the *Medici Venus*, the *Young Apollo*, and the *Grinder* as well as 16th-century Florentine works like the celebrated Medici portraits of *Bartolomeo Panciatichi*, *Lucrezia Panciatichi*, *Maria de' Medici*, the young *Giovanni* and *Bia* by **Bronzino**, *Lorenzo the Magnificent* (1534) by **Vasari**, and *Cosimo the Elder* by **Pontormo**. Observe the splendid *Musician Angel* (1521) by **R. Fiorentino**, the *Madonna of the Well* (1518 ca.) by **Franciabigio**, *Young Woman with the "Petrarchino"* by **A. del Sarto**, and another *Portrait of Eleanor of Toledo with her Son Giovanni* by Bronzino (the dress she wears is the same one she is buried with). At the center of the room there's a table in semi-precious stones from the first-half of the 17th century.

ROOM 19 LUCA SIGNORELLI AND PERUGINO - Here you'll find works like the *Madonna and Child* (1490 ca.) and the *Holy Family* by **Signorelli**, and the *Portrait of Francesco delle Opere* and *Monks* by **Perugino**, the *Annunciation* and the *Venus* by **L. di Credi**, the *Liberation of Andromeda* (1510 ca.) by **P. di Cosimo**, and the *Portrait of Evangelista Scappi* by **F. Francia**.

ROOM 20 DÜRER - Works by German artists (1400s-1500s) are on display here. Look especially for the *Portrait of the Artist's Father* (1490), the *Adoration of the Magi* (1504), the *Madonna della Pera* (1526), *St. Philip* by **A. Dürer**; and the portraits of the *Prince Electors of Saxony* and *Luther*. Observe the ceil-

Botticelli, La Primavera
Botticelli, The Birth of Venus
Leonardo, Adoration of the Magi
Tribuna
Rosso Fiorentino, Musician Angel

ing with paintings on the *Views* of Florence.
ROOM 21 GIAMBELLINO AND GIORGIONE - The works of Venetian painters can be seen here: **Giorgione** with his *Moses' Trial by Fire*, the *Judgement of Solomon*, and the portrait of the *Captain and Squire*; **Giambellino** and his *Sacred Allegory* and *Mourning*; **Cima da Conegliano** with the *Madonna and Child*; **C. Tura** with *St. Dominic*.

ROOM 22 FLEMISH AND GERMAN RENAISSANCE ARTISTS - Works by **A. Altdorfer** (*Stories of St. Florian*, 1530 ca.); **H. Holbein** (*Portrait of Sir Richard Southwell*, 1536, and a *Self-portrait*); **G. David** (*Adoration of the Magi*); **H. Memling** (*Portrait of Benedetto Portinari*, 1487); **J. van Cleve** (*Portraits of a Stranger and his Wife*).
ROOM 23 MANTEGNA AND CORREGGIO - Works by **A. Mantegna**, like the *Madonna delle Cave* (1466), *Portrait of Cardinal Carlo de' Medici*, and the *Triptych*, and by **Correggio**, such as the *Madonna with Child in Glory* (1515) and the *Resting in Egypt* (1517 ca.).
ROOM 24 ILLUMINATIONS - Intended to house the collections of gems and semi-precious stones, it currently gathers the illuminations of Italian and foreign artists (15th-18th cent.). In the SECOND and THIRD CORRIDOR, you'll find

Michelangelo, Doni Tondo
Raphael, Self-portrait
Titian, Venus of Urbino

splendid Roman statues including *Cupid and Psyche*, the *Seated Nymph*, and *Leda*. (*PANORAMIC VIEW)

ROOM 25 MICHELANGELO AND FLORENTINE ARTISTS - Room dedicated to this legendary master and to other 16th-century Florentine artists. You'll see the lovely *Doni Tondo* (1506-1508 ca.) by **Michelangelo** with its original inlaid frame. You'll also see the *Annunciation* by **Fra' Bartolomeo** and the *Vision of St. Bernard* (1507), whereas the *Visitation* is by **M. Albertinelli** (1503).

ROOM 26 RAPHAEL AND ANDREA DEL SARTO - Many works by **Raphael** are located here: the famous *Madonna del Cardellino* (1506), his *Self-portrait*, the *Portraits of the Dukes of Urbino*, *Elisabetta Gonzaga*, and *Giudubaldo da Montefeltro*, and the portrait of *Leo X with Two Cardinals*. The *Madonna of the Harpies* (1517) and *St. James with Children* are by **A. del Sarto**.

ROOM 27 PONTORMO AND ROSSO FIORENTINO - Look for the *Supper at Emmaus* (1525), the *Portrait of Maria Salviati*, and the *Nativity of St. John the Baptist*. There are also paintings by **Bronzino**, Pontormo's pupil: the *Mourning* and the *Panciatichi Holy Family*. **Rosso Fiorentino** is also present especially with his *Portrait of a Girl*.

ROOM 28 TITIAN - Masterpieces by **Titian**, a master painter from the Veneto Region, are on display (his spectacular *Venus of Urbino*, 1538). Other works include *Flora* (1520 ca.), portraits of the Dukes of Urbino, *Eleonora Gonzaga*, and *Francesco Maria della Rovere*, *Portrait of Pope Sixtus IV*, the *Sick Man*, and the *Portrait of a Knight of Malta*. Here you'll also see works by **S. del Piombo,** Michelangelo's friend, like the *Portrait of a Woman* and the *Death of Adonis* (1511 ca.), and by **J. Palma il Vecchio,** also from the Veneto Region, such as *Judith* and the *Holy Family*.

ROOM 29 DOSSO AND PARMIGIANINO - This room is dedicated to **Parmigianino**, a mannerist painter and pupil of Correggio, and his *Madonna with Child and Saints* (1530), *Portrait of a Man*, and the *Madonna dal collo lungo* (unfinished work). You'll also see works by **D. Dossi** such as *Rest during the Flight into Egypt*, *Witchcraft*, and *Portrait of a Warrior*.

ROOM 30 PAINTERS FROM EMILIA - Look especially for the works of **L. Mazzolino** (*Madonna with Child and Saints*, 1522-1523) and **Garofalo** (*Annunciation*).

ROOM 31 VERONESE - This room gathers works by **Veronese**, an artist from the Veneto Region active during the second-half of the 1500s: *Holy Family with St. Barbara and St. John the Baptist* (1564 ca.), *Annunciation*, *Martyrdom of St. Giustina*, *Esther Led to Ahasuerus*. There is also **Vicentino** with his *Visitation*.

ROOM 32 BASSANO AND TINTORETTO - Works by **Tintoretto**: *Adam and Eve before God*, the *Samaritan at the Well*, and *Leda and the Swan*

S. del Piombo, Death of Adonis
Caravaggio, Sacrifice of Isaac
Rubens, Bacchanal
Room of Niobe

(1570 ca.). There are also the portraits of the *Venetian Admiral*, *Jacopo Sansovino*, and a *Man with a Red Beard*. In addition to this artist, there's **Bassano** with his *Two Dogs*.

Room 33 Hall of the Five Hundred - Works by Italian and foreign artists (late 1500s). These include paintings by **F. Clouet** (*Francis I of France on a Horse*, 1540 ca.), **A. Allori** (*Venus and Cupid*), **Vasari** (*Vulcan's Forge*), and **Bronzino** (*Allegory of Happiness*).

Room 34 16th-Century Lombard Artists - Works by **L. Lotto,** an artist who deals mainly with religious themes and is inspired by German artists (*Holy Family and Saints*, *Chastity of Susanna*, 1517, and *Portrait of a Youth*). There's also **G. Campi** and his *Portrait of his Father Galeazzo* and the *Portrait of a Musician*, along with **G. B. Moroni** and his *Portrait of a Learned Man* and *Portrait of Knight Pietro Secco Suardo.*

Room 35 Barocci and the Counter-Reformation - Works by **F. Barocci** like the *Madonna of the People* (1579), and by **Cigoli**, the *Deposition.*

When Buontalenti's grand staircase was reopened, Rooms 36 to 40 were eliminated.

Room 41 Rubens - The paintings of **P.P. Rubens** are shown here and include *Henri IV at the Battle of Ivry*, *Henri IV Enters Paris* (1630), the *Bacchanal*, the *Self-portrait*, and the portrait of his first wife, *Isabella Brant*. You'll also admire works by his pupils: **A. van Dyck** with his *Equestrian Portrait of Philip IV* and that of *Jean de Monfort* (1628 ca.). There is a famous portrait of *Galileo Galilei* (1635) by **J. Suttermans.**

Room 42 Niobe - Sculptures portraying *Niobe* and *Niobides*. This statue, a Roman copy of an original Greek one (2nd-3rd cent. B.C.), was initially displayed in Rome, but later brought to the Uffizi in 1775. Pietro

Leopoldo had a room built to house it. You'll also admire the lovely neo-Attic *Medici Vase* (1st cent.).
ROOM 43 THE ITALIAN AND EUROPEAN SEICENTO - Displayed are beautiful works by **A. Carracci**, such as his *Venus, Satyrs, and Cupids* and the *Self-portrait in Profile*.
ROOM 44 REMBRANDT - Works by the Dutch artist **Rembrandt** are shown here and include his two *Self-portraits* (1634 ca. and 1665 ca.) and the *Portrait of an Old Man*.
ROOM 45 THE ITALIAN AND EUROPEAN SETTECENTO - This room gathers works by **G. M. Crespi** (*Cupid and Psyche*), **P. Longhi** (*Confession*), and by Vedutiste artists like **Canaletto** (*View of the Doge's Palace in Venice*) and **F. Guardi** (series of *Caprices*).
There are also many portraits including the *Presumed Portrait of Marie Adelaide of France Dressed in Turkish Costume* (1753) by **J. E. Liotard**, *Felicia Sartori* by the Venetian artist **R. Carriera**, *Maria Teresa de Vallabriga on Horse* and *Maria Teresa, Countess of Chinchòn* by **F. Goya**.
ROOM OF CARAVAGGIO - Works by Michelangelo Merisi, better known as **Caravaggio**, the celebrated Milanese artist active in Rome between 1593 and 1599, are displayed here. You'll see his lovely *Bacchus*, the *Sacrifice of Isaac*, the spectacular *Medusa* (which is actually a jousting shield that once belonged to Francesco I de' Medici). There's also *Judith Beheading Holofernes* by **A. Gentileschi.**
In the last rooms, you can admire works by B. Manfredi, G. delle Notti, and G. Reni.
There's a great view of the city from the terrace at the end of the corridor. (*PANORAMIC VIEW)

5 MUSEUM OF THE HISTORY OF SCIENCE (Piazza dei Giudici, 1)
Founded in 1927, this museum gathers over 5,000 scientific objects that once belonged to the Medici (the oldest ones date back to Cosimo the Elder) and Lorraine families.
The 2 floors are respectively divided into 11 and 10 rooms. In the exposition areas, you'll find Italian and foreign mathematical instruments (10th-19th cent.), including an Arabian *celestial globe* (1080) and the *armillary sphere* of Antonio Santucci (second-half 1500s). In Rooms 4-5, there are instruments that once belonged to **Galileo Galilei**, like his *objective lens*, with which this great scientist was the first to observe the satellites of Jove, his compass, and telescope. On the floor above you'll find instruments from the 18th-19th centuries.
The *mechanical paradox* is famous. Moreover, you'll see weights and alembics as well as Grand Duke Pietro Leopoldo's work desk and chemical compounds.

3. PONTE VECCHIO and PALAZZO PITTI

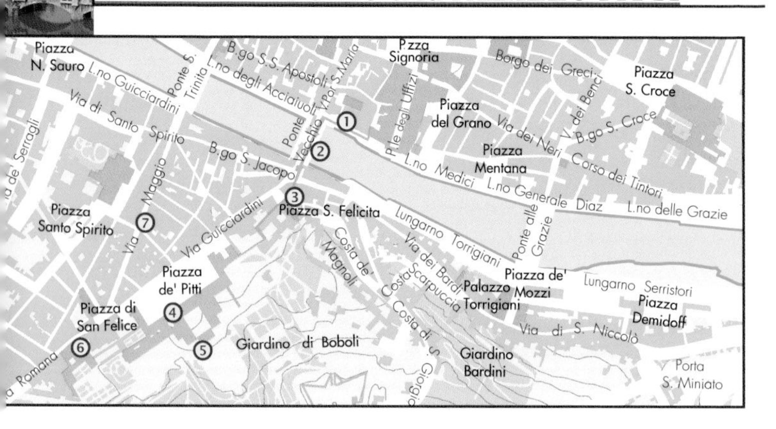

❶ Vasari's Corridor (reservation required)

When the Uffizi was refurbished and enlarged, the Grand Duke asked Vasari to also make a secret passageway that would connect Palazzo Vecchio with the new Grand-Ducal residence, Palazzo Pitti.

This corridor, which was named after its architect (1565), begins inside Palazzo Vecchio, crosses the Uffizi Gallery, continues on top of Ponte Vecchio, and finally finishes, after about 1 kilometer, in the Boboli Garden where Buontalenti's grotto is found.

In 1973, the corridor was converted into an exposition space that today houses about 800 works. The vast *Collection of Self-portraits* of Italian and foreign artists begins in the second stretch (from Ponte Vecchio) and displays works from the 14th century to modern times. Look for the self-portraits of Vasari (1550), Del Sarto, Raphael, Titian, Bernini, Rosa, Canova, Reni, Rubens, Rembrandt,

Velázquez, Liotard, Böcklin, Hayez, Fattori, Michetti, Balla, and Chagall.
As you walk unobserved along the corridor above Ponte Vecchio and cross the tribune of the church of S. Felicita, you'll enjoy some marvelous vistas of the city and the hills. (*PANORAMIC VIEW)

Final stretch of Vasari's Corridor

❷ PONTE VECCHIO
Made up of 3 solid arches, this is the only bridge that has survived since 1345, when it was rebuilt by Neri di Fioravante after the Arno had flooded. Moreover, it is the only bridge that escaped German bombings in 1944. In the late 1500s, Ferdinando I had the shops of the "beccai," Florentine butchers, replaced with goldsmith shops that still today occupy both of its sides. These shops even preserve their original, traditional wooden shop shutters. In one of the 2 terraces, you'll find the *Bust of Benvenuto Cellini*, a 20th-century work. (*PANORAMIC VIEW)

❸ CHURCH OF S. FELICITA (Piazza di S. Felicita)
The church rests upon the foundations of a Paleochristian construction (4th cent.). It is considered the city's oldest sacred construction, even though it was rebuilt

in the 1700s. Vasari's Corridor passes above the entrance portico. Inside, to the right you'll see the *Capponi Chapel*, which might have been designed by Brunelleschi in the early 15th century. Here, you can admire Pontormo's *Deposition* and fresco of the *Annunciation*.

❹ Palazzo Pitti

In the 1400s, Luca Pitti wanted this palace to be built on the Boboli hill so as to challenge the power of the Medici. Designed in 1445 by Brunelleschi, this building initially consisted in a massive ashlar structure with 3 stories (including the 7 central windows) separated by long balconies.
After Pitti died (1473) and his family began to lose power, the palazzo was purchased by Cosimo I for his wife Eleanor of Toledo who moved the court here (1549).
B. Ammannati's first interventions did not greatly alter the façade; instead, the 2 side doors were closed off and replaced with "kneeling" windows, while the palazzo's surface grew in depth. Between 1618 and 1640, 4 more windows were added on each side of the façade by G. and A. Parigi and the interior was embellished. When the Lorraines came to power, G. Ruggeri and P. Poccianti were asked to continue working on this princely residence. Today, it measures 205 meters in length with 2 porticoed side wings called *rotaries*.
Under French domination (1799-1814) the palazzo became the residence of Maria Luisa of Bourbon, Queen of Etruria, and then of Elisa Bonaparte, who had the rooms in the left wing refurbished. In fact, during those years, the artists G. Cacialli and P. Benvenuti set up rooms in Tuscan neo-classical style, like the Bath of Napoleon, though it was never used by the Emperor.

When Florence was Italy's capital (1865-1870) King Vittorio Emanuele also lived here.
Today, 7 art collections are housed inside Palazzo Pitti.
From the central arch-shaped entrance you'll reach Ammannati's courtyard; he also executed the fountain situated above on the terrace, though substituted in 1641 by the famous *Artichoke Fountain* by **F. Susini** and **F. del Tadda**. Below you'll see *Moses' Grotto*, a 17th-century work in porphyry. Lovely Roman statues are located under the portico; to the right you'll find the PALATINE CHAPEL with its mosaic altar and crucifix by Giambologna.
Take the grand staircase. You'll reach the PALATINE GALLERY and the ROYAL APARTMENTS.

PALATINE GALLERY
This collection gathers Italian and European paintings and masterpieces (1400s-1700s). Spread out in various halls, it was begun by Cosimo II in 1620 and later enlarged by Cosimo III. Thanks to the Lorraines, it was opened to the public in 1828. The museum itinerary follows the criterion of private "picture galleries," and therefore the halls are "decorated" by the paintings on display.
HALL OF STATUES OR OF CASTAGNOLI - Named after the artist who painted the room. At the center you'll find the *Table of the Muses* with inlaid semi-precious stones and a bronze stand by G. Dupré (1851).
Next you'll reach the HALL OF ALLEGORIES OR OF "VOLTERRANO": on display are works by **Volterrano** (*The Practical Joke of Father Arlotto*), **G. da S. Giovanni** (*Venus Combing Cupid*), and **Suttermans** (Medici portraits).
Then you'll find other halls that have been converted, in more recent times, into exposition spaces (HALL OF FINE ARTS, OF HERCULES, OF AURORA, OF BERENICE). These gather works (mainly 17th-centu-

ry altarpieces) taken from churches and convents that were suppressed during the 1800s. Next comes the HALL OF PSYCHE dedicated to the works of the Neapolitan artist **S. Rosa** painted during his stay in Florence (1640-1649), especially the *Forest of the Philosophers* and the *Battle.*
Stroll through the rooms set up for Empress Maria Luisa of Bourbon and you'll reach the HALL OF FAME with its Dutch-Flemish works like *Brushwood with Animals* by **O. van Schrieck** and the *Views* by **G. van Wittel**.
Heading back from the HALL OF FINE ARTS you'll come to the HALL OF THE ARK with frescoes by L. Ademollo. This room is pavilion-shaped like the one people thought housed the Ark of the Covenant.
MUSIC ROOM - Also called the "drum" room for the shape of the small furnishings it contains, you'll find a lovely table with a malachite top and stand in gilded bronze.
POCCETTI CORRIDOR - Frescoed by Rosselli, it contains small 17th-century paintings like *Ila and the Nymphs* by **F. Furini**, the *Martyrdom of St. Bartholomew* by **J. Ribera**, the *Three Boys in the Furnace* by **M. Rosselli**. There are also valuable pieces of furniture like the semi-precious stone table designed by **G.B. Foggini** (1716).
HALL OF PROMETHEUS - On display is the *Madonna with Child and Scenes from the Life of St. Anne* by **Filippo Lippi**, the Gallery's oldest painting (1450). You'll also find two panels by **Pontormo**, the *Adoration of the Magi* (1523) and the *Martyrdom of St. Maurice and the Theban Legion*, as well as the *Holy Family with St. Catherine* by **L. Signorelli**. An 1844 Sèvres vase signed by L.P. Schilt is located at the center of the room.
Cross the CORRIDOR OF COLUMNS where small-format Dutch and Flemish works (17th-18th cent.) are housed.
HALL OF JUSTICE - Gathers mainly 16th-cen-

tury works from Venice and the Veneto Region. These include: *Portrait of Tommaso Mosti (?)* by **Titian**, *Portrait of a Gentleman* by **Veronese**, and the *Madonna with St. Catherine and St. John* attributed to **P. Lanciani**.

Hall of Flora - Here you'll find 16th-century Florentine works including the *Holy Family with St. Anne and St. John* by **Vasari** and the *Madonna with Child* by **A. Allori**.

Hall of the Putti - On display are paintings by Flemish and Dutch artists such as *The Three Graces* by **Rubens** and two *Still Lifes with Fruit and Flowers* by **R. Ruysch** (1715 and 1716).

Hall of Ulysses - Frescoed to celebrate Ferdinando III of Lorraine's return to Florence in 1815, it gathers important works such as the *Madonna dell'Impannata* (1514) by **Raphael**, the *Madonna with Child and Saints* (also called "Gambassi Altarpiece," 1525-1526) by **A. del Sarto**, and the *Ecce homo* by **Cigoli** (1607).

Napoleon's Bath - Created in 1813 as Napoleon's imperial apartments, this space is frescoed and decorated with bas-reliefs.

Hall of Jupiter's Education - Originally the Grand Duke's bedroom, it houses the *Sleeping Cupid* (1608) by **Caravaggio**, *Judith with Holofernes' Head* by **C. Allori**, and *St. Andrew before the Cross* by **C. Dolci**.

Hall with Stove - This hall, which got its name from the warm air that was used to heat it, was frescoed with allegorical paintings by P. da Cortona and M. Rosselli. Majolicas adorn the floor.

Hall of the Iliad - Named after its frescoes with images taken from Homeric episodes. It contains works by Raphael, *La Gravida*; **R. Ghirlandaio**, *Portrait of a Lady* (1509); **A. del Sarto,** the *Passerini Altarpiece* and the *Assunta Panciatichi*; **Suttermans**, *Portrait of Valdemaro Cristiano*. You'll also find two paintings by **A. Gentileschi**, *Ju-*

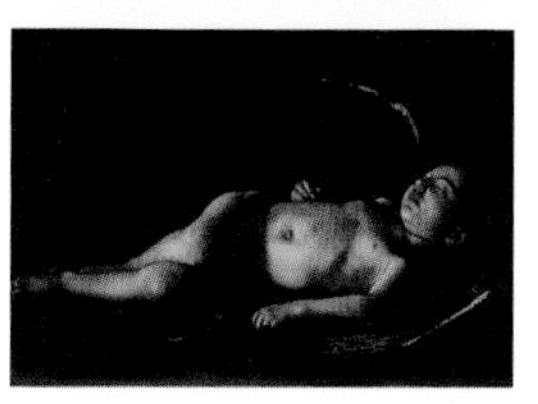

Music Room

Filippo Lippi, Bartolini Tondo

Pontormo, Adoration of the Magi, *detail*

Titian, Portrait of Tommaso Mosti (?)

Raphael, Madonna dell'Impannata

Rubens, The Three Graces

Caravaggio, Sleeping Cupid

Raphael: Madonna della Seggiola; Madonna of the Grand Duke; La Velata
Giorgione, The Three Ages of Man
Throne Room

dith and *Magdalene* (1614-1620).
Hall of Saturn - Frescoed by Ferri, this room contains the most substantial core of Raphael's paintings, including the *Madonna della Seggiola*, the *Portraits of Agnolo* and *Maddalena Doni* (1507), the *Madonna of the Grand Duke* (1506), the *Portrait of Tommaso Inghirami*, and the *Madonna del Baldacchino*, which is unfinished because the painter moved to Rome.
You'll also see *The Disputa on the Trinity* and the *Annunciation* by **A. del Sarto**, the *Lamentation over the Dead Christ* (1495) by **Perugino**, and *Christ as "Salvator Mundi"* (1516) by **Fra' Bartolomeo**.
Hall of Jove - This was originally the throne room, but today it contains the *Holy Family* by **Guercino**, the *Three Ages of Man*, recently attributed to **Giorgione** (1500 ca.), the *Madonna del Sacco* by **Perugino**, the *Pietà* by **Fra' Bartolomeo**, and the *Annunciation* by **A. del Sarto**. But the most celebrated work displayed here is *La Velata* by **Raphael** (1516), made during his stay in Rome; perhaps this work portrays the Fornarina, a woman the artist greatly loved.
Hall of Mars - It contains mainly portraits from the Veneto Region and a few Flemish and Spanish masterpieces. Among the works from Veneto: **Titian**, the *Portrait of Ippolito de' Medici*; **Tintoretto**, the *Portrait of Alvise Cornaro* (1560-1565); **Veronese,** the *Portrait of a Gentleman in a Fur*. Among the Flemish works: *The Effects of War* (1638) and *The Four Philosophers* by **Rubens** and the *Portrait of Cardinal Bentivoglio* by **Van Dyck**. The Spanish are represented by **Murillo** and his two paintings depicting the *Madonna with Child*.
Hall of Apollo - The altarpiece *Sacred Conversation* (1522) by **D. Mazza** dominates the room. You'll also find **Titian** with his *Man with Gray Eyes* or *The Englishman* and *Magdalene*. Other artists from

the same Region are also present: **Tintoretto** with the *Portrait of Vincenzo Zeno* and **D. Dossi** with the *Nymph and Satyr*. There are also works by **G. Reni** (*Cleopatra*), Guercino, and C. Allori. You'll also see Flemish paitings by **Rubens** with his *Portrait of Isabella Clara Eugenia* (1625), **J. Suttermans** with the *Portrait of Grand Duchess Vittoria della Rovere* (1640 ca.), and **Van Dyck** with the *Portrait of Charles I of England and Henrietta of France.*
Hall of Venus - Frescoed with mythological scenes by **P. da Cortona** and **C. Ferri**. It displays works by **Titian** like *The Concert*, the *Portrait of Pietro Aretino*, the *Portrait of a Lady*, the *Portrait of Pope Julius II*; **Rubens** with his *Return of the Peasants from the Fields* and *Ulysses Landing on the Island of the Phaeacians*; **S. Rosa** with his *Seascape at Sunset* and the *Seascape with Ships and Galleys*; **Guercino** and his *Apollo and Marsia*; **Cigoli** with his *Jesus Appears to Peter for the Third Time*. At the center of the room you'll find **A. Canova**'s marble statue *Italic Venus*.

Royal Apartments

Located in the right wing of the palazzo, you can reach this area through the Hall of Niches. This was once the residence of the Medici and Lorraine families. The Savoy family also lived here when Florence was the capital of Italy (1865-1870). In fact, they left most of the furnishings we see today, including lavish tapestries and pieces of furniture. These rooms have been recently rearranged and are divided into 14 areas.
Hall of Niches - The Medici used this hall as a waiting room for visitors. Under the Lorraines, it became a room for festivities and then a dining hall. Here you'll find niches with copies of ancient statues and Japanese vases.
Green Hall - Named after the color of the silk that lavishly covers

Queen's Chambers

Chapel

A. Allori, Vault of the Loggetta dell'Appartamento degli Arazzi

Modern Art Gallery, *Hall of Portraits from the Age of King Umberto I*

the room, it was also called the "Guards' Chamber" because Prince Ferdinando's apartments were located nearby. You can admire a lovely painting by **L. Giordano** with the *Allegory of Peace between Florentines and Fiesolani* and the *Portrait of Fra' Marcantonio Martelli* by **Caravaggio**. This room is sumptuously embellished and also displays a small table with inlaid semi-precious stones and an ebony cabinet (1685 ca.).

THRONE ROOM - Or the "Red" room, it contains a throne, a baldachin, and a balustrade that were placed here at the time of the Savoy family. It was used as a hearing hall under the Medici and the Lorraines. It contains Japanese and Chinese vases (18th-19th cent.).

SKY-BLUE HALL - The silk wall coverings in this hall are sky-blue in color. It was also known as the "Hall of Cymbals" because Grand Prince Ferdinando held concerts here. This stunning room is embellished with stuccos and Gobelins tapestries. You'll also find the 10 portraits of the Medici executed by J. Suttermans (1621-1645).

CHAPEL - Under the Medici it served as a bedroom; in the 1700s, it became a chapel. Note the *prie-dieu*, the altar with an ivory crucifix, and paintings by Titian, Rembrandt, and Van Dyck. **C. Dolci** is credited with the *Madonna and Child* with its lovely frame in tortoise-shell and semi-precious stones.

HALL OF PARROTS - This magnificent room has birds embroidered on the green wall coverings. It separates the rooms of the King and Queen of Savoy. The French clock in gilded chiseled bronze with a black marble base deserves special attention.

YELLOW HALL, QUEEN'S CHAMBERS, OVAL STUDY, AND ROUND STUDY - These were once Queen Margherita of Savoy's apartments, richly adorned with Gobelins tapestries and portraits such as the *Electress Pala-*

tine attributed to **J.F. Douven**. Here you'll find a lovely cabinet in ebony, ivory, alabaster, and gilded bronze, a stoup, and other precious objects.
If you head back to the Hall of Parrots, you'll reach the apartments of King Umberto I of Savoy.
This part is composed of the King's Room, the Study, the Red Hall, and the Anti-chamber. Characterized by furnishings that are less ornate than those found in the other rooms, you'll also find here tapestries, furnishings of the Lorraines, mirrors, a marble bust of the King, portraits by Suttermans.
Apartment of Tapestries - If you go through the Hall of Bona (it was decorated by **B. Poccetti** in 1609 with the *Defeat of the City of Bona*), you'll reach the tapestry room. Composed of 5 rooms set aside for the ladies-in-waiting of the Medici court, it was later used to welcome illustrious guests. Each room was frescoed with personifications of the *Virtues* by the greatest artists during the time of the Medici. Splendid tapestries (French and Tuscan manufacture) depicting allegorical figures hang on the walls. The last hall, the White Room, is decorated with stuccos that brighten up the room.

Modern Art Gallery

In the rooms that were once divided into the Chambers of the Arch Duchesses and the New Chamber under the Medici and the Lorraines, you'll find many noteworthy Italian paintings and sculptures (18th-20th cent.) in addition to some modern masterpieces by foreign artists. The collection was started by Grand Duke Pietro Leopoldo in 1784 and continued under the Savoy family.
Over 2,000 works are arranged in chronological order and divided according to subject matter. The museum is comprised of 30 rooms.

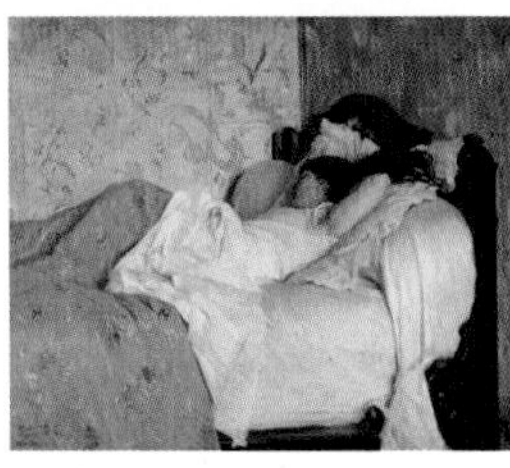

P. Tenerani, Psyche Abandoned

F. Hayez, The Two Foscari

F. Zandomeneghi, In Bed

C. Pissarro, Landscape

G. Fattori, Stepdaughter's Portrait

T. Signorini, Leith

P. Nomellini, Young Bacchus

The first rooms (1–2) are dedicated to neo-classical art and to French occupation in Tuscany. Artists include: **A. Canova** (bust of *Calliope*), F. Carradori, S. Ricci, **P. Batoni** (*Hercules at the Crossroads*), **P. Tenerani** (*Abandoned Psyche*).
In the following rooms (3–4), you'll find paintings dedicated to the iconography of Tuscan dynasties before the unification of Italy, like the Hapsburg-Lorraines and the Bourbons of Lucca (**F.X. Fabre,** the *Portrait of Maria Luisa of Bourbon, Queen of Etruria*), and of the families that contributed in a significant way to Florence, like the Demidoff family (the *Portrait of Princess Matilde Bonaparte Demidoff* by **A. Scheffer**).
Rooms 5 and 6 display historical romantic art and ideal landscapes. You'll find works by **F. Hayez** (*The Two Foscari*), **G. Sabatelli** (*Giotto and Cimabue*), and **M. d'Azeglio** (*Attack of the Cavalry*).
Among the sculptures that can be found here: **P. Fedi** (*St. Sebastian*) and **G. Dupré** (*Little Bacchus of the Cryptogam*).
Rooms 7 and 8 contain commemorative portraits and portraits from when Florence was the capital of Italy. These include: **A. Ciseri** (*Giovanni Dupré*), **R. Sorbi** (*Portrait of the Sculptor Emilio Zocchi*), **A. Puccinelli** (*Portrait of the Noblewoman Morrocchi*), **G. Fattori** (*Self-portrait*).
Room 9 is dedicated to landscape artists from the mid-1800s. Works include: **A. Fontanesi** (*After the Rain*) and **S. De Tivoli** (*A Pasture*).
Rooms 10 and 11 gather two impressive painting collections—that of Cristiano Banti, donated by his heirs in 1958 (works include the *Women of the Woods* by Banti himself), and that of Diego Martelli, donated to the city in 1897 (works include *In Bed* by **F. Zandomeneghi** and *Landscape* by **C. Pissarro**).

The following rooms (12-17) display masterpieces that commemorate historical events, **S. Ussi** (*The Exile of the Duke of Athens*, 1862), and portraits from the time of Umberto I (**M. Gordigiani**, *Portrait of Gabriella Coujère, The Painter's Wife*).

Rooms 18 to 20 gather works by Macchiaioli ("makers of patches") and post-Macchiaioli artists and by artists from other schools. These paintings were formerly held in Municipal deposits or were part of the Ambron Collection. Works by **G. Fattori** (*Stepdaughter's Portrait, Cousin Argia, The Southwesterly Gale*, and *The Palmieri Rotunda*) stand out. Paintings by **T. Signorini** (*September Morning in Settignano, Roofs in Riomaggiore, Leith*) and sculptures by **A. Cecioni** (*The Suicide*) also deserve special mention.

Rooms 21 to 24 display naturalist paintings such as those by **A. Tommasi** (*Spring*) and **G. De Nittis** (*Rain of Ash*). There are also works by artists influenced by European culture (**O. Vermehren**, *Paolo and Francesca*, and **E. Gelli**, *Portrait of Bruna Pagliano*) as well as symbolist and divisionist paintings (the *Little Bacchus* by **P. Nomellini** and *In the Meadow* by **G. Previati**).

Rooms 25 and 26 house collections of studies such as the *Emilio Gagliardini Collection* and include *The Tragic News* by **O. Borrani**, *Horses in the Pinewood of Tombolo* by Fattori, and *Noon* by Nomellini.

The last rooms (27-30) display decadent, symbolist, and post-impressionist works like *Intimacies* by **A. Spadini**, the *Portrait of Giovanni Papini* by **O. Ghiglia**, *Peace* by **G. Chini**, *The Good Smile* by **G. Costetti**.

MUSEO DEGLI ARGENTI (The Grand-Ducal Treasure)

This collection was placed on display in 1919 in the summer apartments of the Medici court so as to house the collection of pre-

cious objects and jewelry gathered over the centuries by the Medici and the Lorraines.
The 25 rooms, some of which are marvelously decorated by G. da San Giovanni (1635 ca.), are mainly grouped according to the type of objects they display (rock crystal, porcelain, amber, ivory, reliquaries, etc.). Make sure you visit the room dedicated to CAMEOS and JEWELRY. You'll find works like the *Cameo of Cosimo I* (1557-1562), the *Ovate with a Perspective of Piazza Signoria* (1599), and the *ex-voto of Cosimo II*; in the EXOTICISMS HALL and the LOGGETTA, you'll find objects from Africa (*ivory horns* from Congo), Mexico (*jade mask*), and China (*nautili*).
The collections of Ferdinando III of Lorraine, called the *Treasure* of the prince-bishops of Salzburg and Würzburg (the portable altar, the series of 54 bowls in gilded silver, and the flask with grotesque art are all impressive), the *Treasure* of Anna Maria Luisa de' Medici (located in the jewelry room and includes some "bejeweled gallantries" with a curious collection of tiny animals from Flanders) as well as Lorenzo the Magnificent's *"Celadon" vases* (14th cent.) can be found here.
The last section of the museum, the HALL OF DONATIONS, gathers jewelry and objects

(1600s-1900s) that were donated to the museum. Here you'll see the splendid *Diadem* by Cartier (1900) studded with amethysts and diamonds.

Carriage Museum (ground floor, temporarily closed to the public)
This museum displays the original carriage models that belonged to the Lorraine and the Savoy families (1700s-1800s), along with saddleries.
The early 19th-century carriage that belonged to Ferdinando II King of Naples stands out. It arrived with the Savoy family and is lavishly decorated in gilded silver.

Costume Gallery
Set up in 1983 in the rooms of the Palazzina of the Meridian (the Savoy family also resided here), this collection gathers over 6,000 items of clothing including centuries-old garments, theater costumes, and accessories (1700s-1900s). Many objects were donated or purchased. The funerary garments of Cosimo I de' Medici, Eleanor of Toledo, and their son Garzia are spectacular.

Porcelain Museum (Casino del Cavaliere, top part of Boboli Garden)
Established in 1973, it collects porcelains that once belonged to the families that lived in Palazzo Pitti. Divided into 3 rooms, Italian and French porcelains are found in the first room (look for the Neapolitan biscuit figurines, and the Doccia and Sèvres tableware). Viennese porcelains are located in the second room, and pieces of Meissen manufacture can be found in the third.

Hall of G. da San Giovanni
Augsburg Manufacture, Cabinet known as "d'Alemagna"
Flask designed by Buontalenti
"Master of the Furies," Curtius Riding his Horse into the Abyss
Silver carriage
Costume Gallery
Doccia Manufacture, Cup

❺ Boboli Garden
This tour ends by crossing the Bacchus Courtyard into the Boboli Garden, which is a fine example of a Renaissance Italian

garden. In 1549, Cosimo I asked **Tribolo** to design this green area, but it took many years to complete. Other architects who worked on the project include Ammannati, Buontalenti, and A. Parigi. It was finally completed in the late 1800s.
The expanse of the garden, 45,000 m. sq. between Palazzo Pitti, Forte Belvedere, and Porta Romana, had to reflect the Prince's power. In fact, this site became the preferred place for court games and performances. Today it offers visitors wonderful vistas of the city. If you stroll through the park, you'll see many statues, fountains, grottos, small ponds, and even an amphitheater. At the garden's ENTRANCE you'll find the curious *Bacchus Fountain* (1560, also called "of the dwarf Morgante") by **V. Cioli** that portrays a dwarf (who resided at Cosimo I's court) on top of a turtle.
BUONTALENTI'S GROTTO (1583-1588) stands out for the originality of its niches; here you'll find the figures of *Paris and Helen*, by **Bandinelli**, with man-made stalactites and marine elements. In the past, Michelangelo's original *Prisoners* were found here (today you'll find the copies), while in the fresco by **Poccetti** you'll see a *Venus* by **Giambologna**.
Don't miss the AMPHITHEATER (17th cent.) right behind Ammannati's courtyard, with aedicules and steps. At the center, you'll find an *Egyptian obelisk* (1500 B.C.) from Luxor and a granite tub from the Baths of Caracalla.
Take the central path and you'll reach a pond with the *Fountain of the Pitchfork* at the center; on the left you'll reach the Kaffeehaus rococo pavilion (1776) that overlooks the city. (*PANORAMIC VIEW)
From the KNIGHT'S GARDEN, with the *Fountain of Monkeys* at the center, head down towards the path that among cypress trees and statues will lead you to the HOLME

SQUARE, a large pond created by G. and A. Parigi beginning in 1618. A sculptural group, portraying various subjects including *Perseus* and *Andromeda* by Giambologna, is immersed in the water, whereas on the central holme, surrounded by a stone balustrade and small lemon trees, you'll find the *Ocean* fountain, a copy of an original by Giambologna. If you head back towards the main exit, you'll see the LAST ROTARY and the LEMON GROVE.

Boboli: *Fountain of the Artichoke and Amphitheater*
Kaffeehaus
Island Pond
Mostaccini Fountain
Grand Grotto

❻ "LA SPECOLA" ZOOLOGICAL MUSEUM (Via Romana, 17)

The Museum was founded in 1775 by Pietro Leopoldo. Here he established an astronomical and meteorological observatory called the "Specola". The Grand Duke aimed to gather in a single location the Medici's scientific collections (including books, treatises, and instruments). In addition to the zoological collections (recently enriched with the purchase of the Italian and African Arachnid collection), the circa 600 display cases contain *the collection of anatomical wax specimens* made by the ceroplastics school, which was located in the museum until 1895.

On the floor above you'll find the famous GALILEO TRIBUNE that Leopoldo I commissioned in 1841 on the occasion of the Conference of Italian Scientists. It is made up of a vestibule and a hemicycle-shaped room decorated with marble, mosaics, and frescoes by various artists.

❼ VIA MAGGIO

Among the 16th-century palazzos, look for no. 26. Here you'll find the *palazzo of Bianca Cappello* (lover and second wife of Francesco I de' Medici); it was refurbished for her by B. Buontalenti and presents on its façade graffitoed grotesque art and a traveler's hat, the family's coat-of-arms.

4- OLTRARNO and S. TRINITA

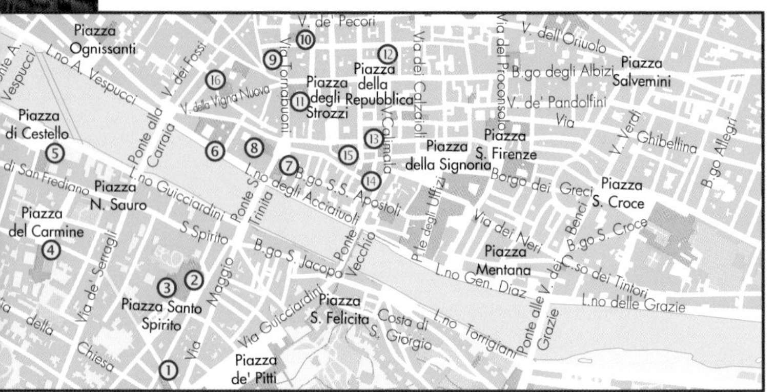

❶ Church of S. Felice in Piazza

Mentioned in documents as early as 1066, the church as it appears today dates back to the 1300s. The unadorned façade, attributed to **Michelozzo**, and the sculpted portal stand out. Some of the works inside include: on the SIXTH altar to the right you'll find the painting *Madonna and Saints* (1520) by **R. del Ghirlandaio**; in the MAIN CHAPEL, a wooden *Crucifix* (Giotto school) and to the left, the fresco *St. Felix Helping St. Maximus*, begun by **G. da S. Giovanni** and completed by **Volterrano** in 1636.

Piazza S. Spirito

The square, surrounded by 15th-century palazzos, resembles a garden with a fountain at the center and it comes to life especially in the summer thanks also to the presence of many traditional restaurants nearby. Look for Palazzo Guadagni, a 16th-century construction that was perhaps designed by **Cronaca** for the Dei family; in fact, it served as

❷

a model for many palazzos that were built for the large arcaded loggia situated above.

Palazzo Guadagni

Church of S. Spirito: *A. Sansovino, Sacrament Altar*

Filippino Lippi, Madonna with Child and Saints

❷ Church of S. Spirito

The church's unadorned 18th-century façade faces the square. The church was begun in 1444 by **Brunelleschi,** but completed by his successors in 1487 when the dome was built. In the late 1400s, other famous artists like **G. da Sangallo** (sacristy) and **Cronaca** (vestibule) also worked here. The slender, two-story bell tower, topped by an elegant belfry, was finished in 1541 and designed by **B. d'Agnolo**, whereas B. Ammannati and A. Parigi completed the complex with the two cloisters between the 16th and 17th centuries.

The church INTERIOR is shaped like a Latin cross with 3 naves. The large dome is located at the center of the transept.

If you begin your visit from the RIGHT NAVE, you'll come across works from the 15th to 17th centuries. These include: CHAPEL IV, *Jesus Driving the Merchants out of the Temple* (1572) by **G. Stradano; G. Caccini**'s MAIN ALTAR with its marble enclosure and a dome-covered baldachin is Baroque in style and has semi-precious stones; heading towards the apse you'll see a wooden *Crucifix* attributed to **Michelangelo**. CHAPEL XII houses the lovely work by **Filippino Lippi** entitled *Madonna with Child and Young St. John, St. Martin, and St. Catherine Martyr* (1494). In CHAPEL XIV, you'll find the marble sarcophagus dedicated to Neri di Gino Capponi, attributed to Bernardo Rossellino (1458). In the APSE, CHAPEL XVII displays the polyptych by **M. di Banco**, *Madonna with Child and Four Saints* (1345 ca.), whereas CHAPELS XIX and XX contain two signed and dated works by **A. Allori**, *The Martyr Saints* (1574) and *The Adulteress* (1577).

In the LEFT TRANSEPT you'll find, among the most important works, those in CHAPEL

XXVI, such as the *Enthroned Madonna with Child and St. Thomas and St. Peter* by **C. Rosselli** (1482). The lovely CHAPEL XXVII, also called CORBINELLI CHAPEL, presents architecture and furnishings by **A. Sansovino** (1492). In CHAPEL XXX, there's the *Enthroned Madonna with Child and Saints* by **R. del Garbo**, embellished with a splendid period frame.
Proceed to the LEFT NAVE. CHAPEL XXXIV, with the *Madonna, St. Anne, and Other Saints* by **R.** and **M. del Ghirlandaio**, is of particular interest. Look above to see the magnificent 15th-century stained glass windows. You'll be able to access the VESTIBULE from a door located under the organ. This was built by **Cronaca** (1494) and is shaped like a rectangle with a coffered barrel vault depicting mythological figures and supported by 12 Corinthian columns.
The SACRISTY (access from the vestibule) is the work of G. da Sangallo and was built between 1489 and 1492. It contains paintings like the one on the altar facing the entrance, *St. Fiacre Heals the Sick* (1596) by **A. Allori**. In the FIRST CLOISTER (access from the vestibule), the frescoed lunettes portraying *Stories of Augustinians*, executed by various artists, stand out.

3 CENACOLO DI **S. SPIRITO** (Piazza S. Spirito, 29)
This 14th-century Augustinian refectory is noteworthy for its rectangular shape and for its exposed truss covering with Gothic mullioned windows. On one of the walls you'll find the splendid fresco with overlapping scenes of the *Crucifixion with Mary, The Pious Women, Longinus and Other Soldiers*, and the *Last Supper* (1365 ca.), attributed to **Orcagna**, though unfinished in a few sections.
The FONDAZIONE ROMANO is also located here. This collection was donated to the city in 1946 by the antiques dealer Salvatore Romano; it includes statues, fragments of architecture, and other

precious objects from pre-Romanesque times to the 15th century.

❹ Church of S. Maria del Carmine

The church, founded by the Carmelites in 1268, still bears the ruins of a Romanesque-Gothic structure. The church was refurbished over the centuries, and was finally completed in 1775 by G. Mannaioni. The INTERIOR, with its frescoed ceilings, is in the shape of a Latin cross with 1 nave and 5 chapels on each side with decorated altars. Special mention must be made of CHAPEL III with its *Crucifixion* (1560) by **Vasari**.

In the MAIN CHAPEL, with its *ciborium* in marble and semi-precious stones, you'll find the *funerary Monument of Piero Soderini*, a sculpture by **B. da Rovezzano** (1513). From the LEFT TRANSEPT you'll reach the *Corsini Chapel*, a square-shaped, Roman Baroque-style room completed in 1683 by P.F. Silvani for Marquis Bartolomeo and Neri. Three funerary monuments are located inside, as well as many works by **G.B. Foggini**, including the *urn* with the body of S. Andrea Corsini.

Brancacci Chapel (access from the door to the right of the church) - The chapel is especially renowned for its frescoes by **Masaccio** and **Masolino**.

Orcagna, Last Supper, Crucifixion, *Cenacolo di S. Spirito*

Church of S. Maria del Carmine: Masaccio and Filippino Lippi, Resurrection of the Son of Theophilus and St. Peter on His Throne

Corsini Chapel

Felice Brancacci commissioned these works to Masolino and Masaccio in around 1423. Both artists worked together on this project up until 1428 (ca.). With the banishment of Felice Brancacci (1436) and Masaccio's untimely death, the work continued slowly. It was then decided that the chapel would be dedicated to the *Madonna of the People*. In fact, the 13th-century panel portraying the *Madonna*, which can sill be found on the altar, was brought here. This work is attributed to **C. di Marcovaldo**.
Filippino Lippi completed the frescoes in 1480; the themes of the *Original Sin* and *Episodes from the Life of St. Peter* follow one another. Certain scenes deserve special mention: *Temptation of Adam and Eve* by **Masolino**; the highly dramatic *Expulsion from the Garden of Eden* by **Masaccio** is considered the starting point of Renaissance painting. Next you'll see the most celebrated episode of the entire cycle: *Tribute Money* by Masaccio. Then: *St. Peter Preaching* by Masolino; the *Baptism of the Neophytes* by Masaccio; the *Resurrection of the Son of Theophilus and St. Peter on His Throne* by Masaccio and Filippino Lippi. This is considered the last episode Masaccio painted before he moved to Rome; the portraits of many of his contemporaries are rather interesting. Look for Brunelleschi, Alberti, Masaccio, and Masolino. The final scenes are by Filippino: *The Dispute with Simon Mago*, *The Crucifixion of St. Peter* (you can see the painter's self-portrait in the first episode—he is the young man with a hat on the far right; instead, in the second episode you'll find the *portrait of Sandro Botticelli*, Filippino's teacher—he is the person at the center of the group on the right who looks at the observer), and finally the *Angel Freeing St. Peter from Prison*.

5 Church of S. Frediano in Cestello

This church, with its unfinished façade, was built between 1680 and 1689 by the Roman architect Cerutti. It is adorned with a dome by A. Ferri (1698) and a bell tower. The INTERIOR, in the form of a Latin cross with 1 nave, stands out for its Baroque style and small side chapels. A must-see: the dome's decorations by D. Gabbiani and the impressive 18th-century MAIN ALTAR in marble and semi-precious stones. In the LEFT TRANSEPT, you'll find the *Crucifixion and Saints* by **J. del Sellaio**.

7

6 PALAZZO CORSINI AND GALLERY (Lungarno Corsini, 10) (*PANORAMIC VIEW)
Designed by P.F. Silvani (1656), this palazzo is home to the CORSINI GALLERY collection (visits must be scheduled in advance), begun in 1765 by Father Lorenzo Corsini. It contains masterpieces by artists from Florence, Italy, and abroad (1400s-1700s).

8

7 PALAZZO SPINI-FERONI
Erected in the late 1200s to defend the bridge, you'll be amazed by this massive, three-story, embattled construction. It was refurbished various times and, until 1824, it also had a tower and an arch. Since 1995 the SALVATORE FERRAGAMO MUSEUM has been located here; this museum contains 10,000 shoe models created by the maison from the 1920s to today. Historical documents like films and photos round off the collection.

8 BASILICA OF S. TRINITA
This church is located in Piazza Santa Trinita. At the center of the square you'll find the *Column of Justice*. The basilica was built by Vallombrosian monks in the second-half of the 11th century. It was later enlarged and modified in Gothic style during the early 1300s. Work was finally concluded in the early 15th century. The Baroque stone façade was designed by B. Buontalenti. The INTERIOR has a Gothic layout in the form of an Egyptian cross with

L. della Robbia, Tomb of Benozzo Federighi

D. Ghirlandaio, Sassetti Chapel

3 naves. In the RIGHT NAVE, CHAPEL IV stands out: it is closed off by an iron gate and contains frescoes by **L. Monaco** (1425) depicting *episodes from the Virgin's life*. This same artist also executed the panel with the *Annunciation* located on the ALTAR.
In the RIGHT TRANSEPT, in the *Sassetti Chapel* you can admire the cycle of frescoes by **D. Ghirlandaio** with *Stories of St. Francis of Assisi* (1486). Important figures of the age (Francesco Sassetti and his son, Lorenzo de' Medici, Agnolo Poliziano with the Magnificent's children) and sights such as Piazza S. Trinita, Palazzo Spini, and Palazzo della Signoria can be seen. Take note of Ghirlandaio's *Adoration of the Shepherds* on the altar.
In the PRESBYTERY, few fragments of a cycle painted by A. Baldovinetti of stories taken from the Old Testament can be seen. In the LEFT TRANSEPT, in CHAPEL II, look for the *Tomb of Benozzo Federighi, Bishop of Fiesole* (1454) in marble with multi-colored majolica tiles by **L. della Robbia**. The CHAPEL WITH THE RELICS OF ST. GIOVANNI GUALBERTO, decorated by **Passignano** with scenes related to the veneration of this saint's relics, is right nearby.
In the LEFT NAVE, in CHAPEL V, the wooden statue depicting *Magdalene* by **D. da Settignano** is rather impressive. Make sure you stop by CHAPEL IV to see the tomb of the medieval Florentine chronicler Dino Compagni.

❾ VIA DE' TORNABUONI

This is Florence's most elegant and famous street with fashionable shops and lovely Renaissance palazzos. Look for: *Palazzo Minerbetti* (Via de' Tornabuoni, no. 3), *Palazzo Strozzi del Poeta* (no. 5), an example of Baroque architecture by **G. Silvani**, *Circolo dell'Unione* (no. 7) by **Vasari** but based on a project by **Giambologna**, *Palazzo Corsi* (no. 16), a 15th-century building by **Michelozzo** with a loggia refurbished by **Cigoli** in 1608.

⑩ Church of S. Gaetano (Piazza Antinori)
Dedicated to the order of the Theatins, this church is an exquisite example of Baroque art (1638). The interior is covered in black marble.

⑪ Piazza and Palazzo Strozzi
The palazzo of the merchant Filippo Strozzi the Elder was built here in the late 1400s. **B. da Maiano**'s project consisted in a cube-shaped structure with ashlar work and 3 identical sides. It was Cronaca who carried on the project between 1502 and 1503, adding the protruding cornice and the courtyard with a collumned arcade and loggia. Refurbishment, however, was definitively suspended in 1538. In fact, the south façade and half of the cornice were never completed. Take note of the wrought iron finishings like the flag and horse poles, iron lamps, and bands for torches and banners around the construction
Today, this palazzo is State property. A few of the halls have been set aside for exhibitions. Also located here is the *Gabinetto G. P. Vieusseux*. Founded by the Swiss merchant Giovan Pietro Vieusseux in 1819, it possesses a vast library (about 650,000 volumes) open to the public as well as a restoration workshop.

⑫ Piazza della Repubblica
This square was built between 1885 and 1895 on top of the centuries-old constructions of the Mercato Vecchio and in the area that once was the Roman forum. Overall, the square today seems like an elegant open-air lounge area with its very refined cafés. However, this square was originally home to the Jewish ghetto, Vasari's Loggia del Pesce (today located in Piazza dei Ciompi), and various private residences.

Il porcellino, *Loggia of the Mercato Nuovo*

Lo Scheggia, Il gioco del civettino, *Museum of the Ancient Florentine House*

V. Micheli is also credited with the triumphal arch and its series of porticos. In 1951, the *Column of Abundance* was erected here; this column marks the spot where the Roman *decumanus* and *cardus* once met.

⓭ LOGGIA OF THE MERCATO NUOVO (New Market)

Also called the Loggia *of straw* or *del Porcellino* for the fountain that portrays a boar (a bronze copy of the original by **P. Tacca)**. The loggia, square in shape, was commissioned by Cosimo I to G. B. del Tasso (1551). Goods from the most important guilds of the age would be sold here. During the 19th century, statues were added to beautify the loggia. Today, you'll find many stands that sell handmade Florentine products.

⓮ PIAZZA DI PARTE GUELFA

A small medieval section of the center, the former church of Santa Maria Sopraporta (today a library) and the PALAGIO DEI CAPITANI DI PARTE GUELFA, which was formerly the headquarters of the magistracy of Guelph captains, are located here. The 14th-century building was enlarged by Brunelleschi and Vasari and refurbished in the early 1900s. Today, the

Calcio Storico Fiorentino has its offices here. It also hosts various temporary exhibitions and cultural events.

⓯ Palazzo Davanzati (Piazza Davanzati)

Museum of the Ancient Florentine House - It was built by the Davizzi family (merchants) in the 1300s, but passed on to the Davanzati family in 1578, who lived here until 1838. After various owners, this palazzo became State property and in 1956 a museum was opened here. What might catch your eye are the iron objects on the façade that were once used to tie horses, "erri," or rather, rods used to hang laundry or bird traps, and torch or flag holders on the sides of the windows. This museum displays furnishings (chests, beds, credenzas, tables, refectory chairs), paintings, statues, tapestries, and everyday objects (basins, pitchers, plates, lamps, looms, irons) of a typical 14th-century family. The lively decorations on the walls will certainly delight you. Make sure you see the Parrot and Peacock Rooms.

⓰ Piazza de' Rucellai

Shaped like a triangle, this square was designed by L.B. Alberti during the second-half of the 1400s. Palazzo Rucellai, built in various phases between 1455 and 1470 by B. Rossellino and designed by Alberti himself, looks out onto the square. The Alinari photo archives and the Fratelli Alinari Museum of Photography History (now in Largo Fratelli Alinari, 15) were once located here. This museum gathers antique cameras and photo equipment and hosts temporary photo exhibitions. In front of the palazzo you'll see the Loggia de' Rucellai with 3 arches with the family's coats-of-arms (rings with diamonds and feathers and sails); in the past, family celebrations were held in this loggia.

5. S. MARIA NOVELLA and OGNISSANTI

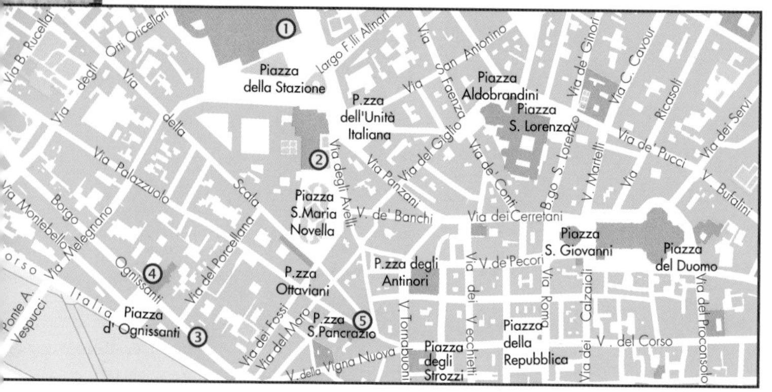

❶ S. Maria Novella Train Station

The train station is located behind the Basilica of S. Maria Novella. It was built between 1933 and 1935 and is based upon a project by the "Gruppo Toscano," directed by G. Michelucci. It was intended to be a modern structure in *pietra forte* in perfect harmony with the centuries-old constructions surrounding it. The inside roof is made of glass; the floor is in marble and serpentine and there are many benches, baggage rests, and small bronze drinking fountains. You'll find 2 tempera landscape paintings by **O. Rosai** on the walls.

Piazza S. Maria Novella

This is one of the loveliest squares in Florence. It was begun in 1287 by will of the commune and completed around 40 years later. It acted as the center of religious activities and public life (the *palio dei Cocchi*, a horserace that involved riding around the 2 marble obelisks supported by 4 turtles made by Giambologna, was held here starting in 1563).
Facing the square are the Church of S. Maria Novella and the Loggia of the Hospital of S. Paolo, a 13th-century foundation offering medical assistance; it was suppressed by Grand Duke Pietro Leopoldo in 1780. Between the arches of the building you'll find glazed terracotta medallions depicting saints by **A. della Robbia**.

❷ Basilica of S. Maria Novella

The origins of this complex date back to 1221 when a few Dominican friars took up residence in the church of S. Maria delle Vigne (11th cent.). A new church was then built in 1278. The work, carried out by the friar architects Sisto and Ristoro, were completed in the mid-14th century. Even though the Gothic

façade remained incomplete, the church was consecrated by Pope Martin V in 1420. On the occasion of the 1439 Council, plans were made to finish the façade, and with funds from the wealthy Florentine, Giovanni Rucellai, Alberti was entrusted with the task. He integrated the already-present Gothic elements into his typically Renaissance design. The result is exceptional. In fact, there is a continuity of color and proportion. Observe the beautiful triangular tympanum with a sun, the symbol of the Dominicans. Among the details Alberti added there are the frieze with the name of Giovanni Rucellai and the date, 1470, as well as the family's coat-of-arms. In 1574, a gnomon on the right and an armillary sphere on the left were added.

The INTERIOR, transformed various times, is in the shape of a Latin cross with 3 naves divided by columns in *pietra forte*. It's one of Florence's most prestigious sights for the quantity and quality of its art (works by Giotto, Orcagna, Brunelleschi, Masaccio, and Filippino Lippi). You'll find an endless succession of chapels. Some of the most important ones include: RIGHT NAVE: (bay II) *Tomb of the Blessed Villana* (1451) by

Filippo Strozzi Chapel

F. Brunelleschi, Crucifixion
Giotto, Crucifixion
Masaccio, Trinity
Green Cloister

B. Rossellino and **D. da Settignano**; (bay VI) Chapel of the Pure, built by the Ricasoli family in 1473 to house the miraculous image of the Madonna, venerated by Florentine mothers. At the end of the nave on the right, go up the steps and you'll reach the Rucellai Chapel: on the altar you'll find the *Madonna with Child*, a marble sculpture by **N. Pisano** (mid-14th cent.). In the transept on the right, you'll see the Bardi Chapel with its iron gate and lamps from the 1700s; there's also a painting on the right pillar of *St. Gregory Blessing the Founder of the Chapel*, while on the altar you'll see the *Madonna of the Rosary* (1570) by **Vasari**. In the Filippo Strozzi Chapel, decorated with frescoes (1502) by **Filippino Lippi**, observe the *Tomb of Filippo Strozzi* by **B. da Maiano**. In the main chapel or the Tornabuoni Chapel, dedicated to Our Lady of the Assumption, you'll see the *cycle of frescoes* (1490) by **D. del Ghirlandaio** and in the sacred scenes (including the *Life of the Virgin*, *Stories of St. John the Baptist*, the *Evangelists*), you'll recognize many famous figures of the age. Under the paintings there's the inlaid wooden *chorus* by **B. d'Agnolo**. On the altar you'll find a bronze *Crucifix* by **Giambologna**. The Gondi Chapel, covered with marble and porphyry by **G. da Sangallo** (1503), is famous for the *Crucifix* by **Brunelleschi**, this artist's only work in wood. Then there's the Gaddi Chapel, in marble and semi-precious stones and decorated with frescoes depicting the *Episodes from the Life of St. Jerome* and the *Virtues* by **A. Allori**. In the left transept, you'll find the Strozzi Chapel (of Mantua) with *frescoes* (1350-1377) by **N. di Cione** inspired by Dante's *Divine Comedy*, which is represented on the left; on the altar, there's the panel *Christ Risen Giving the Keys to St. Peter and a Book to St. Thomas, the Madonna, St. John the Baptist,*

and Other Saints (1357) by **Orcagna**. In the Gothic SACRISTY, observe the lavabo in marble and glazed terracotta by **G. della Robbia**, relic cabinets designed by Buontalenti, and a wooden *Crucifix* by **Giotto** at the entrance. In the LEFT NAVE (bay IV), look for the *Trinity* fresco with the *Madonna, St. John, and the Patrons Lenzi Kneeling Down* by **Masaccio** (1427 ca.), a fundamental work in which the artist applied the teachings of Brunelleschi's mathematical perspective. Nearby you'll also see a lovely marble *pulpit* (1462) by Brunelleschi.

S. MARIA NOVELLA MUSEUM OF SACRED ART AND THE CLOISTERS
This museum is chiefly composed of the cloisters and the refectory annexed to the basilica.
GREEN CLOISTER: Built by **Fra' J. Talenti** (1332-1350 and after) and surrounded by lowered round arches, it was frescoed by **P. Uccello** with *Creation Stories* (1425-1430) using mostly green paint. Observe the *Creation of the Animals*, the *Original Sin*, *Noah's Ark*, the *Universal Flood*, and the *Drunkenness of Noah.*
CAPITUALR HALL OR SPANISH CHAPEL - In 1540, Eleanor of Toledo created this chapel for the many noble Spaniards in her court; it's rectangular in shape with a single cross vault held up by large arches. The vault and the walls are frescoed by **A. di Buonaiuto** with a cycle depicting the zealous activity of the Dominicans in combating heresies. Some episodes include *St. Peter Sailing*, the *Resurrection*, the *Pentecost*, the *Militant and Triumphant Church*, and the *Triumph of St. Thomas Aquinas.*
CLOISTER OF THE DEAD - This area was already present when the friars arrived. It is a colonnade on 2 sides with octagonal pillars and cross vaults. Here you'll find the *funerary chapel of the Strozzi family* with frescoes by Orcagna's pupils.

P. Uccello, Episodes from the Genesis and the Life of Noah
A. di Bonaiuto, Triumph of St. Thomas Aquinas, *Spanish Chapel*
D. Ghirlandaio, Last Supper
Botticelli, St. Agustine in His Study

Refectory - It hosts the Museum of Sacred Art where you'll see objects that belonged to the Dominican friars. These include paintings, reliquaries, sacred wall hangings. Look for the sinopia by **P. Uccello**, the bust-reliquaries of St. Orsola, the rock crystal display case with the relic of the Title of the Cross, and the *Last Supper* (1584) by **A. Allori**.
Main Cloister and the Popes Chapel - These two areas are occupied by the School of Petty Officers and can be visited only upon authorization. The chapel hosted Pope Leo x de' Medici in 1515 and was frescoed on that occasion by **R. Ghirlandaio** and **Pontormo**, who painted the *Veronica* here.

❸ Borgo Ognissanti

Walking along this street, try to find no. 26. Here you'll see the *Casa-galleria* (House-Gallery), created in 1911 by the architect **G. Michelazzi,** a rare example of art nouveau architecture in Florence.

❹ Church of Ognissanti

The most important construction in Piazza Ognissanti is the church founded in 1251 by the order of the Humiliati, dedicated wool weavers. Due to its proximity to the Arno and many mills and workshops, this was an ideal site for the friars' activity.
The bell tower is medieval, whereas the façade, refurbished in 1637 by M. Nigetti, is Baroque. Observe the city's emblem and the lunette above the portal with the *Crowning of Mary and Saints* in glazed terracotta.
The interior consists in a single nave with a transept. On altar ii to the right, you'll find frescoes by **D. Ghirlandaio** depicting the *Pietà, Deposition from the Cross*, and the *Madonna of Mercy*. On altar iii there's the panel of the *Madonna and Saints* by **Santi di Tito** (1565), and then the lovely fresco by **Botti-**

celli, *St. Augustine in His Study* (1480 ca.). Almost in front of this work you'll see *St. Jerome in His Study* by Ghirlandaio. In the CHAPEL after altar I in the right transept, you'll find on the floor the marble tomb of Botticelli and his family, the Filipepi.

The MAIN ALTAR (1593-1595) was made by **J. Ligozzi** in semi-precious stones; the bronze *Crucifix* is by **G. B. Cennini** (17th cent.).

In the SACRISTY, observe the fragments of 14th-century frescoes by **T. Gaddi** and the painted *Cross* (Giotto's pupils). The religious complex ends with a cloister and refectory where you can admire a *Last Supper* by **Ghirlandaio**.

❺ MARINO MARINI MUSEUM (Piazza di S. Pancrazio)

Inaugurated in 1988 in the former Church of S. Pancrazio, it gathers the collection of the artist **Marini** (1901-1980). The former church was divided into 3 floors, and the works were arranged according to year and theme. Paintings include *The Virgins* (1920), an oil on canvas clearly influenced by Piero della Francesca and Masaccio, the *Lansquenet*, the *Jugglers* (1954). Don't miss the following works: *Victory* (1928, plaster cast), the *Swimmer* (in wood), the *Horse* (in bronze), and *Anita* (1943, in terracotta).

6. S. LORENZO and the MEDICI CHAPELS

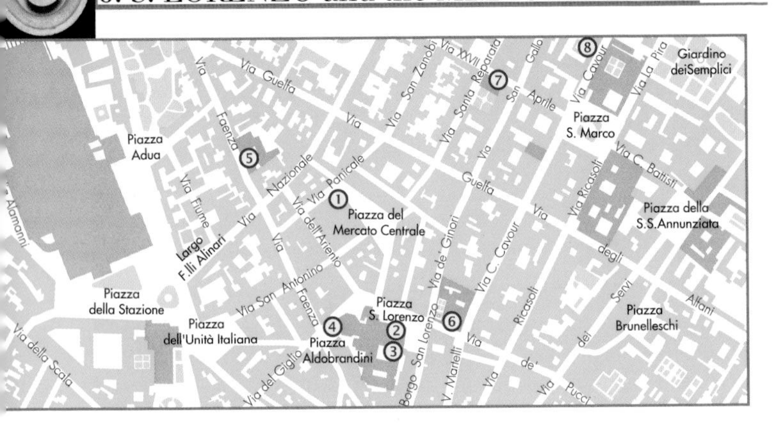

❶ Market of S. Lorenzo

One of the most important glass and iron structures built by G. Mengoni in 1874, it was intended as a place where food could be bought and sold. It exists even today.

Piazza S. Lorenzo

This vast square, famous for its market, is set off by the Church of S. Lorenzo and by lovely palaces (15th-16th cent.) including the celebrated *Palazzo Lotteringhi della Stufa* (no. 4). In front of the church you'll see the *Monument to Giovanni of the Black Bands* (1540), a Medici family forefather, by **B. Bandinelli**.

❷ Basilica of S. Lorenzo

Consecrated in 393 by St. Ambrose, it is dedicated to the martyr Lawrence. It was the city's first cathedral until the 8th century. The

basilica was rebuilt in Romanesque style and re-consecrated in 1059. In 1418, the Medici family became its official patrons and decided to completely refurbish it at their own expense and with contributions from other powerful families in the area, who would then be given a chapel inside the basilica. The work was commissioned to Brunelleschi, who presented his designs in 1421 to Giovanni de' Medici, the city's Gonfalonier. The church was completed in 1461. A library and the mausoleum of the Chapel of Princes were then added. The INTERIOR, despite the 19th-century refurbishment, is harmonious with its decorations in *pietra serena*. This basilica houses rather important works. Starting in the RIGHT NAVE observe CHAPEL II: *Marriage of the Virgin* (1523) by **R. Fiorentino,** and between the last chapel in the right nave and the transept you'll find the marble *Altar of the Sacrament* (1460 ca.) by **D. da Settignano**. Under the 2 final arches of the central nave you'll admire 2 bronze *pulpits* by **Donatello**; these are in the shape of an ark that rests upon Ionic columns. In the MAIN CHAPEL: the semi-precious stone altar made by the Opificio delle pietre dure (1787). LEFT TRANSEPT, CHAPEL I: wooden sculpture

R. Fiorentino, Marriage of the Virgin

Donatello, Resurrection Pulpit

Old Sacristy

P. and F. Tacca, Monument to Ferdinando I

by **G. Fetti** portraying the *Madonna with Child*. In CHAPEL II, observe the altarpiece, the *Abbot St. Anthony on a Throne with St. Lawrence and St. Giuliano*, from the workshop of **D. Ghirlandaio**.

OLD SACRISTY - You'll reach the Old Sacristy from the back of the left transept. It was built by Brunelleschi (1421-1426) as a chapel for Giovanni de' Medici. Decorations were entrusted to Donatello who created the *bas-reliefs* with angels, the large lunettes above the entrances, the lavabos depicting (on the right) *St. Cosmas and St. Damian* (patron saints of the Medici family) and *St. Lawrence and St. Stephen* (on the left), the *tondos* on the walls with the *Evangelists*, and the *pendentives* with *Stories of St. John the Evangelist*. At the center of the room you'll see the *tomb of Giovanni di Bicci de' Medici and his wife Piccarda Bueri* by **A. il Baggiano**, with festoons, angels, and the Medici coat-of-arms. To the left there's the funerary monument to Piero and Giovanni de' Medici, Cosimo the Elder's son, dating to 1472; it is chiseled in porphyry by Verrocchio. On the apse vault, the position of the painted stars indicates the date July 4, 1442. Once you're back inside the church, look for the CHAPEL OF ST. COSMAS AND ST. DAMIAN, also called the Chapel of "the Relics." Here you'll find the reliquaries of Lorenzo the Magnificent. MARTELLI CHAPEL: the last in the left nave, it displays the altarpiece by **Filippo Lippi** depicting the *Annunciation*. FIRST CLOISTER - This first cloister, with its garden, contains many tombstones of men of letters and members of noble families.

❸ MEDICI-LAURENTIAN LIBRARY (access from the cloister)

Built starting in 1524 by Michelangelo for Pope Clement VII de' Medici so as to house the library begun by Cosimo the Elder. The collection is composed of numerous precious manuscripts including a Greek-Egyptian papyrus (3rd cent. B.C.) and striking illuminated codices. Work was completed in 1568 by Ammannati and Vasari. The READING ROOM has benches and reading desks. Observe the lovely ceiling in inlaid wood (1550) and the terracotta floor with a similar decorative motif.

4 MEDICI CHAPELS (Piazza Madonna degli Aldobrandini, 6)
These include the CHAPEL OF PRINCES and the NEW SACRISTY. This construction was conceived by Cosimo I as a mausoleum intended to commemorate the Medici dynasty. It was completed by M. Nigetti (1644) under Ferdinando I.
First you'll see Buontalenti's CRYPT where 4 niches with the bodies of the Medici and Lorraine Grand Dukes (such as Giovanni of the Black Bands and Anna Maria Luisa) are kept. Underground (open only on special events) you'll see the *Tomb of Cosimo the Elder* by **Verrocchio** and *the tombstone of Donatello*. Walk up the steps and you'll reach the chapels. This octagon-shaped room is topped with a dome frescoed in 1828 with *Stories of the Old and New Testaments*. The decorations on the walls, which are covered with semi-precious stones and marble made by the Opificio delle Pietre Dure, are striking. In the splendid, you'll find emblems in semi-precious stones, lapis lazuli, coral, and mother-of-pearl of the Tuscan cities ruled by the Grand Dukes. Members of the Medici family, from Cosimo I to Cosimo III, are buried here. Every sarcophagus was supposed to contain the statue of the prince, but only the ones belonging to Ferdinando I and Cosimo II (in gilt bronze) by P. and F. Tacca were actually made (17th cent.). TREASURE OF LORENZO: near the altar you'll find in 2 rooms the reliquaries, including rock crystal vases, of Lorenzo the Magnificent.
NEW SACRISTY
After passing through a hallway, you'll reach the New Sacristy, which was started in 1520 by Michelangelo. He had been commissioned by Pope Leo X to create an area that would gather the tombs of Lorenzo the Magnificent's family. The work encountered many ups and downs, but was finally completed by Ammannati and Vasari (1555). The room is square-shaped and topped with a dome. Below the *Madonna with Child* (1521) by Michelangelo you'll find the tomb of Lorenzo de' Medici and his brother Giuliano. Next comes the *Monument of Giuliano, Duke of Nemours*, and upon the sarcophagus you'll see the figures of *Day* (on the right) and *Night* (on the left) with symbols representing nighttime like the poppy flower and the screeching owl. On the wall opposite you'll find the *Monument of Lorenzo, Duke of Urbino* (1533), the Magnificent's grandson, depicted as a leader deep in thought. The statues of *Dawn* and *Dusk*

Michelangelo: Tomb of Giuliano de' Medici, Duke of Nemours;
Tomb of Lorenzo de' Medici, Duke of Urbino;
Madonna with Child

Palazzo Medici Riccardi: Courtyard of Michelozzo

B. Gozzoli, The Procession of the Magi, *detail*

rest upon this tomb. An altar with a bronze *Crucifix* attributed to **Giambologna** is also found here.

❺ CENACOLO DEL FOLIGNO (Via Faenza, 40)
It once was a convent for the nuns of Foligno. This complex is important because in the refectory or the HALL OF THE CENACOLO, you'll see a lovely *Last Supper*. This is based upon a drawing by **Perugino** and was made by his pupils.

❻ PALAZZO MEDICI RICCARDI (Via Cavour, 1, former Via Larga)
Today, the Prefecture and various administrative offices are located here. This palazzo was once the residence of the Medici family at the start of their social ascent. In 1437, Cosimo the Elder asked **Michelozzo** di Bartolomeo to build his new residence here. On the façade look for the mullioned windows with the Medici coat-of-arms, whereas at the corners you'll see not only the large Medici coat-of-arms, but also the one of the Riccardi family, who purchased this palazzo in 1659. The Riccardi family enlarged the building by adding a new wing, though maintaining the same types of forms. COURTYARDS - The first place to visit is the courtyard made by Michelozzo with a portico and Corinthian columns. Here you'll see part of the *Riccardi Collection*, which contains about 300 archeological finds. The second courtyard has now become a garden with statues and lemon trees.

CHAPEL OF THE MAGI
Take the steps on the right (built by G. B. Foggini). You'll arrive in the magnificent CHAPEL OF THE MAGI frescoed by **B. Gozzoli**. This room is square-shaped and has a small tribune for the altar where you'll see an altarpiece depicting the *Nativity*. The walls were decorated with episodes of the *Procession of the Magi*, in relation

to the altarpiece image, in 1460. In fact, if you look closely, you'll be able to make out Giuliano, Lorenzo's brother (on the left, the young man riding a horse with a lynx) and Piero the Gouty (portrayed on the right among the group of knights who follow Lorenzo the Magnificent in his gilded armor). Galeazzo Maria Sforza is portrayed on horseback with a gold star on his head, whereas Gozzoli himself is shown wearing a red hat with "Opus Benotii" written on top in gold. Don't miss the HALL "OF THE FOUR SEASONS" with its beautiful 17th-century tapestries, and the typically Baroque GALLERY made by P. M. Baldi; here you can admire the *Madonna with Child* by **Filippo Lippi** (1452 ca.). The **RICCARDIAN LIBRARY** (entrance from Via de' Ginori, 10) is annexed to the palazzo. Opened to the public in 1715, it gathers approximately 4,000 manuscripts including the illuminated *Virgilio riccardiano*, 700 incunabula, and over 50,000 volumes.

7 CENACOLO DI **S. APOLLONIA** (Via XXVII Aprile, 1)
This room was once the convent refectory of the Benedictine nuns of St. Apollonia (founded in 1339). Once it became State property, in 1891 it was converted into the ANDREA DEL CASTAGNO MUSEUM, an artist who painted the walls with frescoes and sinopie in 1444. Some of the most beautiful scenes include the *Resurrection*, the *Crucifixion*, and the *Last Supper*.

8 CHIOSTRO DELLO SCALZO (Via Cavour, 69)
This cloister gets its name from the cross bearer of the Compagnia dei Disciplinati di S. Giovanni Battista who would walk barefoot during processions. It was frescoed by **A. del Sarto** in the early 1500s with *Stories of St. John the Baptist*. Two scenes were completed by **Franciabigio** in 1518.

7. S. MARCO and the ACCADEMIA GALLERY

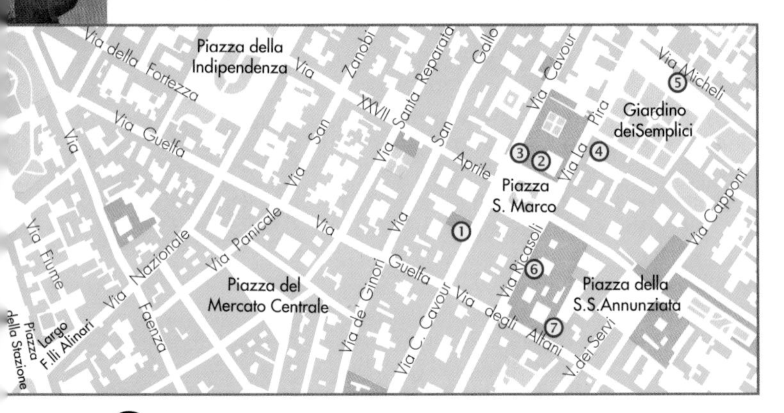

❶ Marucellian Library (Via Cavour, 43)
This important library was established between the 17th and 18th centuries by the abbot of noble origins, Francesco Marucelli. It was opened to the public as early as 1752 and contains an enormous patrimony of circa 554,000 volumes, 2,574 manuscripts, and 30,405 letters and documents.

❷ Church of S. Marco (Piazza S. Marco)
In 1437, Cosimo the Elder asked Michelozzo to enlarge the primitive 13th-century Romanesque-Gothic convent. It was later consecrated in 1443. Angelico, Fra' Bartolomeo, St. Antonino (Bishop of Florence), and above all the preacher Girolamo Savonarola lived here. The church's façade was altered various times (in 1780 it was adorned in Baroque and late Baroque style). The INTERIOR also underwent many transformations: composed of a single nave, work was done by Giambologna during the 1500s (side chapels), and Silvani modified the tribune and the ceiling in the 1600s. On the COUNTER-FAÇADE, you'll see a *Crucifix* by a pupil of Giotto and on ALTAR I to the right there's *St. Thomas Praying in front of the Crucifix* (1593) by **Santi di Tito**. On ALTAR II, you'll find the *Madonna and Saints* by Baccio della Porta (more commonly known as **Fra' Bartolomeo**), and on ALTAR IV there's *St. Zanobus*, sculpted by **Giambologna**. In the SACRISTY by Michelozzo, on display are a *sarcophagus* in black marble with a bronze St. Antonino attributed to Giambologna and the *Bishop's vestments of St. Antonino* designed by **A. Allori** (16th cent.). The frescoes of the dome, which was completed in 1712, are by **A. Gherardini**. On the main altar look for a *Crucifix* (1425-1428) by **Angelico**.
From the presbytery you'll reach the SERRAGLI CHAPEL or the SACRAMENT CHAPEL with frescoes by Santi di Tito and **B. Poccetti**. The

nave on the left side opens with the CHAPEL OF ST. ANTONINO or the SALVIATI CHAPEL, frescoed by **G. B. Baldini. Passignano** is credited with the frescoes found in the VESTIBULE. Instead, the bronze bas-reliefs with *Episodes from the Life of St. Antonino* are by Giambologna. Once you're back in the church, visit ALTAR III and you'll find the tombs of the humanists *Giovanni Pico della Mirandola* and *Poliziano.*

❸ MUSEUM OF S. MARCO

A section of the convent was converted into a museum after 1866. You'll reach the museum by passing through the CLOISTER OF ST. ANTONINO, created by Michelozzo and decorated with frescoes depicting *St. Dominic Kneeling in front of Jesus on the Cross* by Beato Angelico. This artist's work can also be seen in the HALL OF HOSPICE, which was once used to host poor pilgrims. Among Angelico's most beautiful works: the *Deposition of Christ* (1432), the *Altarpiece of St. Mark* and of *Annalena*, the *Tabernacle of the Linaioli*, with its lovely 12 musical angels and the treasure closet with 35 images of the *Stories of Christ*. In the CAPITULAR HALL, you'll see a fresco by this same artist that portrays a *Crucifixion and Saints* (1442), as well as a wooden *Crucifix* (1496) by **B. da Montelupo**. Observe the bell known as the "Piagnona" because it sounds like the followers of Savonarola (called Weepers) when he was captured by Medici soldiers in 1498. From here you'll reach the HALL OF THE CENACOLO frescoed by **D. Ghirlandaio** with the *Last Supper* (1480 ca.). On the ground floor there are other rooms including the HALL OF THE LAVABO with a lunette by P. Uccello, paintings by Fra' Bartolomeo and M. Albertinelli, and the *Madonna with Child* in glazed terracotta by **L. della Robbia**. The HALL OF FRA' BARTOLOMEO is dedicated to this artist who

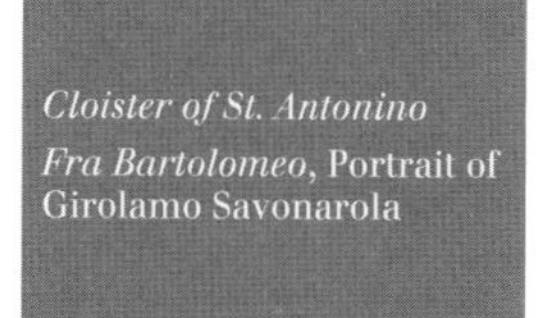

Cloister of St. Antonino

Fra Bartolomeo, Portrait of Girolamo Savonarola

painted the *Last Judgement* (1499) and the *Portrait of Girolamo Savonarola*.
The FLOOR ABOVE is composed of 3 corridors located one after the other around the cloister of St. Antonino. The 43 monk cells are located here. Angelico, assisted by his pupil B. Gozzoli, created a *frescoed cycle* between 1442 and 1445 (the sinopie are probably his) for this area. The most important scenes include the *Annunciation* (signed, 1440 ca.), the *Crucifixion*, the *Crown of Thorns*, *Noli me tangere*, and *Christ Transfigured*. In cell 25, you'll find the *Madonna of the Shadows*. In the THIRD CORRIDOR, **Gozzoli** is attributed with *Christ Is Tempted*, the *Oration in the Garden*, and the *Adoration of the Magi* painted in Cosimo the Elder's private cell. You'll also find the entrance to the LIBRARY where 115 illuminated codices by celebrated artists (including Angelico and D. Ghirlandaio) are displayed in turns.

❹ **MUSEUM OF NATURAL HISTORY** (Via G. La Pira, 4)
This museum derives from the one founded in 1775 by Grand Duke Pietro Leopoldo of Lorraine. The collection is so vast that objects have been grouped into various categories and are displayed in numerous locations throughout the Province. Here

you'll find the collections of the Museum of Mineralogy and Lithography (about 45,000 mineral fragments), the Museum of Geology and Paleontology (about 300,000 fossil and rock specimens and a Tertiary mammal), and the Botanical Museum (founded in 1842 by Filippo Paratore), which is the most important exposition of its kind in Italy.

❺ **Giardino dei Semplici or Botanical Garden** (Via P.A. Micheli, 3, seasonal opening)
This is an open-air museum that extends over 2 hectares. It was created by Cosimo I de' Medici in 1550 and was designed by Tribolo, though it was successively modified. Among the centuries-old trees, don't miss the yew Micheli planted in 1720. Over 6,000 species of plants from across the world can be admired here.

❻ **Accademia Gallery** (Via Ricasoli, 60)
Founded by Pietro Leopoldo in 1784 as a workshop for young Accademia delle Arti students, it gathered only 14th-16th-century Florentine works in so far as they were considered excellent examples of good art. When convents and confraternities were suppressed in the late 1700s, a great number of religious paintings arrived in this gallery, though this practically stopped

B. Angelico, Annunciation; Deposition of Christ; The Mocking of Christ, the Virgin and St. Dominic; Tabernacolo dei Linaioli

Accademia Gallery: *Michelangelo*, David

Gallery

Russian School, St. Catherine

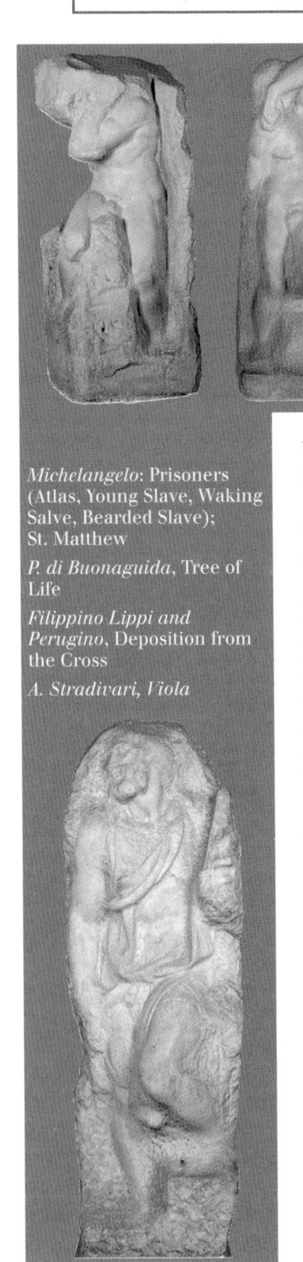

Michelangelo: Prisoners (Atlas, Young Slave, Waking Salve, Bearded Slave); St. Matthew

P. di Buonaguida, Tree of Life

Filippino Lippi and Perugino, Deposition from the Cross

A. Stradivari, Viola

when **Michelangelo**'s *David* was moved here in 1873. Some of Michelangelo's other masterpieces was acquired during the course of the 20th century. A collection of plaster casts from 19th-century sculptors and of Russian icons from the private collection of the Lorraines were also added.

Hall of the Colossus - The second of the 9 halls that comprise the museum. Here you'll find the original plaster model of **Giambologna**'s *Rape of the Sabines*. Paintings include the *Mystical Wedding of St. Catherine* by Fra' Bartolomeo and the *Deposition from the Cross* by **Filippino Lippi** and **Perugino**.

Gallery - Michelangelo's four *Prisoners* (1530 ca.) are located here. These unfinished sculptures were intended for the great mausoleum of Pope Julius II in Rome. However, Michelangelo's nephew gave these works to Grand Duke Cosimo I who placed them inside Buontalenti's grotto in the Boboli Garden. They were later moved to the Gallery. The subjects of the statues are: the *Young Slave* and the *Bearded Slave* on the right, and the *Waking Slave* and *Atlas* on the left. To the right of these *Prisoners* you'll also find *St. Matthew*, placed here in 1831; this sculpture was part of an unfinished series of Apostles that were supposed to be placed inside the

chorus chapels of the Duomo. You can also admire the *Pietà di Palestrina* (1550 ca.); however, there is still some uncertainty regarding the attribution of this work.
The *David* is located at the back of the Gallery in the neo-classical tribune that was made to house it (1882). This grandiose statue (4.10 meters h.) was sculpted by Michelangelo (1501-1504). The image of David was chosen because it has always been a symbol of Florence and it represents shrewdness that defeats brute force. This work was intended for the Tribune in the Duomo, but it was instead placed in front of Palazzo Vecchio as a reminder of civil and political liberties. In the arms of this Tribune, you'll also find other works including the *Venus and Cupid* (1535 ca.) by **Pontormo** (but designed by Michelangelo). *Christ Entering Jerusalem* by **Santi di Tito** and the *Disputa over the Immaculate Conception* by **C. Portelli** are also worth seeing.
FLORENTINE ROOMS - Fifteenth-century Florentine paintings are on display here. Look especially for the majestic *Cassone Adimari* (*Dance Scene*) by **Scheggia** with the accurate reproduction of a wedding procession around the Baptistery, the *Thebaid* attributed to **P. Uccello,** the *Madonna with Child, St. John the Baptist, and Two Angels* (1468 ca.) by **Botticelli**, and the soave *Madonna of the Sea* attributed to Filippino Lippi. The *Resurrection* by **R. del Garbo** is among the most important altarpieces on display here.
THE BARTOLINI COLLECTION OF PLASTER CASTS - This room was set up in 1985 with the signed plaster casts created by Lorenzo Bartolini, the most important sculpture teacher at the Accademia di Belle Arti during the 19th century.
GIOTTESQUE HALL - Also referred to as the "Byzantine" hall because you'll find pre-Giottesque paintings here. Observe the lovely panel depicting the *Tree of Life* by **P.**

Museum of the Opificio delle Pietre Dure:
Work desks with wooden tools and showcases with stones
Cabinet door with sunflower
Medici coat-of-arms

di Buonaguida and the 22 tiles by **T. Gaddi** designed around 1333 and once found in the Church of S. Croce.

TOP FLOOR ROOMS - Set up in 1985, these 4 rooms gather Florentine paintings from the 14th to 15th centuries such as the *Annunciation* and the predella for the altarpiece of S. Trinita by **L. Monaco** as well as the Gothic-style *Annunciation* by the **Maestro della Madonna di Strauss**. Room III contains the collection of Russian icons that once belonged to the Lorraines. On the ground floor you'll find the EXPOSITION OF MUSICAL INSTRUMENTS of the Luigi Cherubini Conservatory (adjacent to the Accademia), which includes rare pieces that belonged to the Medici and the Lorraines. A must-see: the precious Stradivarius violins.

7 MUSEUM AND OPIFICIO DELLE PIETRE DURE (Via degli Alfani, 78)

The Opificio, or workshop, was established in 1588 by Ferdinando I de' Medici. It was moved from the Uffizi to its present-day location in 1796. Here you'll find works in semi-precious stone and *scagliola* as well as inlaid mosaics. An interesting collection of rocks is also displayed.

The Opificio delle Pietre Dure is a museum that is both unique and absolutely pe-

culiar to Florentine art. The love and tradition for this type of manufacturing dates back to the early Renaissance.
Born at the Medici court, the passion for objects in semi-precious stones can be seen as early as the 15th century in prized collections of cameos and ancient gems and vases. In the 16th century, the Grand Duke founded a workshop in order to revive this typically Florentine form of art.
In 1588, Ferdinando I established the "Galleria dei lavori" (Gallery of Works). Initially, various Milanese masters specialized in cutting rock crystal worked here, but later on Florentines and other artisans from Northern Europe were admitted. It was a veritable melting pot of artistic styles.
The Grand-Ducal Gallery soon refined the art of the "commesso," or rather, mosaics made with semi-precious stones cut up into various shapes and sizes and then arranged with such precision that the finished object would resemble "a painting in stone."
Tables, cabinets, jewelry boxes, chessboards, paintings, and ecclesiastical objects (a sublime example is the Prince's Chapel) were painstakingly executed with very thin pieces of semi-precious stones. Still lifes, landscapes, portraits, genre scenes, coats-of-arms took shape as differently colored stone chips were placed next to one another. In fact, the skilled artisans of these inlaid mosaics played with the effects the color combinations produced. The objects became even more precious as they were assembled and finished off by artisans specialized in working with bronze, enamel, and ebony.
Over the centuries, the Gallery's creations enriched the Medici residences, but rulers from the most important courts in Europe also coveted these precious objects, which became status symbols. The art of the "commesso," therefore, distinguished Florentine art in the world; it was a symbol of the power and prestige of the Medici, and afterwards of the Hapsburg-Lorraines, who ruled Tuscany beginning in 1737.
The Opificio kept up production until the late 1800s. It then began restoring works of art. The Museum is born from the history of this magnificent place and the people who worked here. In addition to important objects in inlaid mosaic, the Museum displays various collections of rare stones the Grand Dukes intended for the use of the Opificio, drawings, models, and instruments for working semi-precious stones. All these bear witness to 3 unforgettable centuries of art history.

8. SS. ANNUNZIATA and OSPEDALE degli INNOCENTI

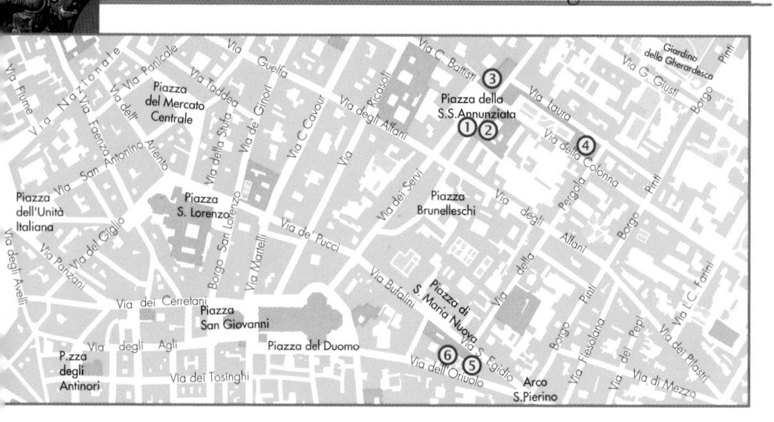

❶ Piazza SS. Annunziata

This area was an important center for social gatherings as early as the 13th century. In fact, the weekly market (on Saturdays), the feast of the Annunciation (March 25, which also corresponded to the beginning of the Florentine year), and the popular "Rificolona" (festivities in honor of Mary's birth that are still held on the night between September 7 and 8. According to tradition, worshipers pay homage to the Virgin by entering the church with a wooden pole and an attached lantern) were all held here. At the center of the square you'll find the *Equestrian Statue of Grand Duke Ferdinando I* (1608), begun by **Giambologna** and completed by **P. Tacca**. There are also two fountains with sea monsters (1629) by Tacca.

Brunelleschi re-elaborated the square during the second-half of the 1400s. He designed the two loggias that set off the church:

the loggia of the Ospedale degli Innocenti (1419) and the one opposite the Confraternità dei Servi di Maria, also called the *Loggiato dei Serviti* (begun in 1516 and designed by A. da Sangallo the Elder and B. d'Agnolo).

❷ Ospedale degli Innocenti

On the right of the square you'll find the institute, important in past centuries, that educated children who had been abandoned in the "rota," a rotating stone located at the opposite end of the portico. Begun in 1419 and financed by the powerful Silk Guild, the Ospedale was inaugurated in 1445. The architect created a perfect symmetry for the portico spaces. In 1487, 8 tondos in white and blue glazed terracotta by A. della Robbia portraying newborn babies in swaddling bands were placed in the pendentives between the arches. The vault and the lunettes were frescoed by B. Poccetti.

D. Ghirlandaio, Adoration of the Magi

Cloister of the Ex-Votos

Cloister of Men - This cloister, completed in 1470, leads to the picture gallery. Observe the decorations with the emblems of the Silk Guild (door), the hospital of S. Maria della Scala (stairs), and the Hospital of S. Gallo (rooster).

Picture Gallery - Here you can admire mostly sacred works: the *Madonna with Child and an Angel* by a young **Botticelli**, the *Madonna with Child* (1450) in glazed terracotta by L. della Robbia, and the *Madonna degli Innocenti* by **F. Granacci**.

❸ Basilica-Sanctuary of the SS. Annunziata

Founded in 1250 by the friars of the Servi di Maria order, it was intended as a small oratory dedicated to Mary. It was later enlarged (1444-1477) and given a round domed, tribune begun by Michelozzo and completed by L. B. Alberti. Under the por-

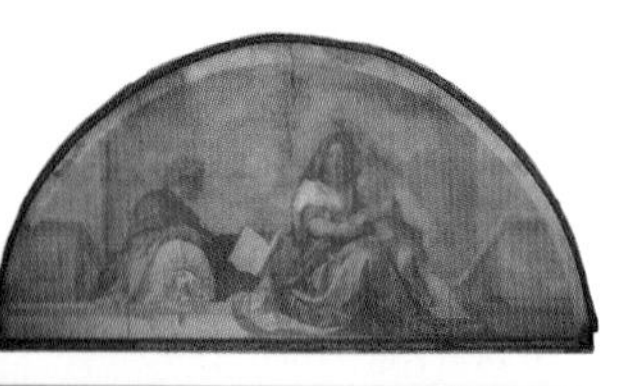

A. del Castagno, The Holy Trinity and St. Jerome, St. Paula, and St. Eustace

Chapel of the Annunciation

A. del Sarto, Madonna del Sacco

tico you'll find 3 doors: the one in the middle will lead you to the CLOISTER OF THE EX-VOTOS; here, ex-votos were hung up until 1780. Also observe the gallery of Renaissance frescoes: the *Nativity of Mary* (1514) and the *Arrival of the Magi* (1511) by **A. del Sarto** as well as the *Marriage of Mary* (1513) by **Franciabigio**, the *Visitation* (1514-1516) by **Pontormo**, and the *Assumption* (1517) by **R. Fiorentino**. Two bronze stoups by **A. Susini** (1615) and the *Stories of S. Filippo Benizzi* by A. del Sarto can also be admired.

INTERIOR - It has a single nave and is mainly Baroque in style, especially its decorations: on the ceiling you'll find a painting (*Our Lady of the Assumption*) by **Volterrano** (1664-1670). Try to visit, on your left, the CHAPEL OF OUR LADY OF THE ASSUMPTION, with its marble, small-temple shape and bronze gate. Here you'll also find many ex-votos and a particular silver altar where the *Annunciation* is displayed (this was especially venerated by married couples because it supposedly brought good luck). Other chapels you should try to see include, in the LEFT TRANSEPT, CHAPELS II and III with frescoes (1456) by **A. del Castagno** depicting *S. Giuliano*; CHAPEL IV with the *Last Judgement* by **A. Allori**; CHAPEL V and the *Assumption of Mary* by **P. Perugino**. In the CHAPEL OF RELICS, on the right towards the sacristy, you'll see the tomb of the artist Passignano, who decorated this chapel and was buried here in 1638. Observe the PRESBYTERY and its round tribune shape and 9 chapels (designed by Michelozzo). The decoration is Baroque and the ciborium and the silver frontals on the main altar are rather splendid. Under the choir in the chapel you'll see two *angels* by **Empoli**; in CHAPEL IV, there's the *Resurrection* by **A. Bronzino**. CHAPEL V, also called the MADONNA DEL SOCCORSO CHAPEL, is entirely dedicated

to the works of Giambologna. In the RIGHT TRANSEPT, CHAPEL VIII, observe the *Crucifix* (1450 ca.) attributed to A. del Castagno and the marble sculpture group of the *Pietà* by **B. Bandinelli**, who is buried here and who portrayed himself in the figure of Nicodemus. There are also many funerary monuments such as the *Tomb of Marquis Luigi Tempi* (1849) by **U. Cambi**, the tomb and bust of **G. Stradano** (1605), and the *Funerary Monument of Bishop Angelo Marzi Medici* (1546) by **F. da Sangallo**.
CLOISTER OF THE DEAD - You'll arrive here from the left transept (please ask the sexton first). The lunette frescoes with *Stories of the Servants of Mary* were executed by various artists including Poccetti. **A. del Sarto** is credited with the lovely *Madonna del Sacco* (1525) located above the church entrance.
CHAPEL OF THE COMPAGNIA DI S. LUCA - To the right of the cloister; the Compagnia was a 14th-century institution of Italian and foreign artists. In 1563, Cosimo I gave it the title of Accademia delle arti del Disegno, which was located here until 1784. In the vestibule, observe the wooden *Crucifix* by **A. da Sangallo**, while inside you'll see on the altar *St. Luke Painting the Madonna* by **G. Vasari**. On the right observe the *Trinity* by **A. Bronzino**, and on the left, the *Madonna with Child and Saints* by **Pontormo**.

❹ NATIONAL ARCHEOLOGICAL MUSEUM (Via della Colonna, 38)
Located in the *Palazzo della Crocetta*, built by G. Parigi in 1619-1621 for Grand Duchess Maria Maddalena of Austria. This collection is the most important in Italy for its Etruscan finds and is second, after the National Archeological Museum in Turin, for its Egyptian artifacts. In the garden, admire some Etruscan tombs (like *tholoi* and chamber tombs) re-constructed with material found in the early 1900s.

ETRUSCAN MUSEUM
This collection was begun by Cosimo the Elder and Lorenzo the Magnificent and includes gems, works in bronze, and coins. Many donations and acquisitions over the centuries greatly enriched the collection. The ground floor is dedicated to the ETRUSCAN-GREEK-ROMAN ANTIQUARIUM where you'll see many Etruscan funerary sculptures. Also on display: the *François Vase*, an Attic *krater* (540-530 B.C.), the cinerary urn *Mater Matuta* (460-450 B.C), who was the goddess of maternity and fertility, and the *Sarcophagus of Larthia Seianti* (2nd cent. B.C.), depicted as she brushes aside her veil to look at herself in a mirror. In the rooms dedicated to ETRUSCAN FUNERARY SCULPTURE, finds mostly from Volterra, Chiusi, and Perugina are displayed. You can't miss the

Sarcophagus of Larthia Seianthi

Chimera

Sarcophagus of the priest Khonsumes

G. Utens, Belvedere with Pitti, *"Firenze com'era" Museum*

numerous urns, especially the *Sarcophagus of the Amazons* (4th cent. B.C.) in marble. Observe also the famous *Small Idol* statue representing a young libating man and the celebrated *Chimera* (4th-5th cent. B.C.), a three-headed monster with a lion's body found in Arezzo in 1553. The Etruscan statue depicting the *Haranguer* (early 1st cent. B.C.) is also noteworthy. The Ceramics Collection, which gathers Greek and Etruscan vases with black and red figures, and the Glyptic Collection, containing Roman and Renaissance cameos and Hellenic and Roman gems, are also worth seeing.

Egyptian Museum

This museum was established between 1824 and 1828 by Leopoldo II of Lorraine. The collection was later enriched and presently contains over 15,000 finds.
Objects are arranged according to date and area of provenance. The time period ranges from prehistory to the late New Kingdom. Don't miss the *Shery Stone Slab* (2500-2200 B.C.) and the *Hippopotamus*, a symbol of fertility. The *Head of Queen Tiy*, wife of Amenophis III (1403-1365 B.C.), is from Karnak. Funerary objects include the *Wooden Cart* from the necropolis of Thebes. The *Bas-relief of the Goddess Maat* dates to the New Kingdom. The section dedicated to funerary papyri with chapters and scenes from the *Book of the Dead* is rather impressive. The *Funeral Trousseau of Amenhotpe* and the *Heart Beetles* date to the 18th-19th dynasties, whereas the 2 stele with an indication of when the tomb was purchased date to the Ptolemaic period.

5 Florentine Museum and Institute of Prehistory (Via S. Egidio, 21)

Established in 1946, the collections date from the Stone Age and come from exca-

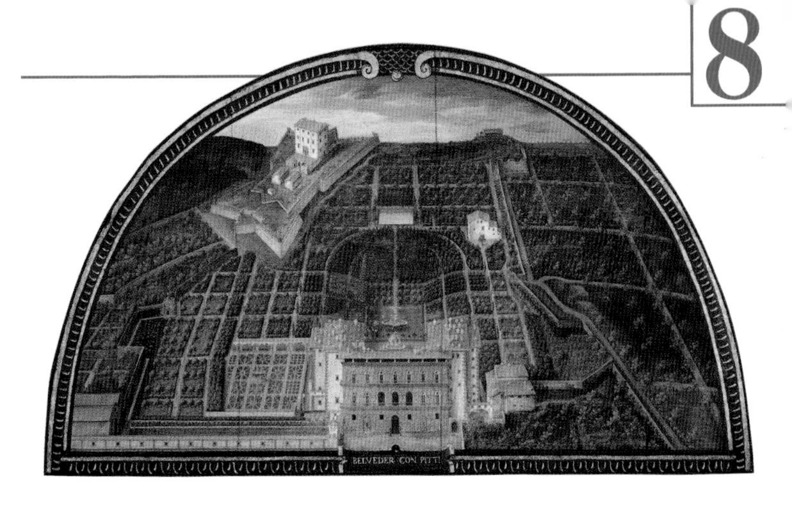

vations in Europe, Africa, America, and Asia. Here you'll find tools made in stone or bone, ceramics, bronze and copper weapons, and the remains of plants and animals.

❻ "FIRENZE COM'ERA" MUSEUM (Via dell'Oriuolo, 24)
This museum was established in 1908 and was later moved to its current location. It documents Florence's evolution and transformation over the centuries. It chiefly gathers lapidary fragments from the various demolitions of the city's historic center, drawings, prints, photos, and etchings. Numerous works are on display and include the 19th-century painting *Map known as "della Catena"* (1470), a map of Florence by **S. Buonsignori,** the 12 *Views of Medici Villas* (1599), tempera on panel by **G. Utens**, the 24 prints with *Views of the City* (1754), and 50 others with *Views of Florentine Villas* (1744) by **G. Zocchi**.

If you get a chance, try to visit the CHURCH OF **S. MARIA MADDALENA DEI PAZZI** (13th cent.) located in Borgo Pinti, no. 58; it is preceded by a cloister where you can admire frescoes by L. Giordano and a *Crucifixion* by **Perugino** (1496). The 19th-century **JEWISH TEMPLE** (Via L.C. Farini, 4) is decorated in Byzantine and Moorish style and has a great dome in light-blue copper. It also has Venetian mosaic frescoes on the inside. The **HOSPITAL OF S. MARIA NUOVA** (Piazza S. Maria Nuova) is the oldest hospital in Florence and is still open to the public; it was founded in 1288 by Folco Portinari, the father of Dante's beloved, Beatrice. The CHURCH OF S. EGIDIO houses the *Tomb of Folco Portinari.* The **TEATRO DELLA PERGOLA** (Via della Pergola, 12), inaugurated in 1718, is one of Florence's most prestigious theaters.

9. S. CROCE and the BARGELLO

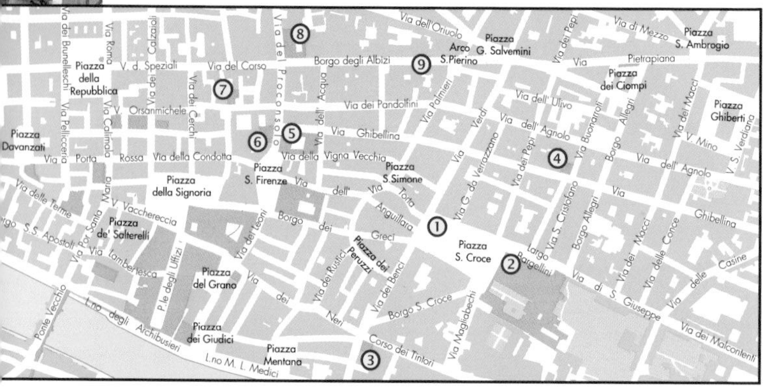

Church of S. Croce: *Main Chapel*

Giotto, Funeral of St. Francis, *detail*

❶ Piazza S. Croce

This square was built during the Middle Ages in the area outside the second ring of walls. People would assemble in this piazza to hear sermons given by the Franciscan friars or to participate in public events and games, like jousts or soccer matches (even today the entertaining games of the Calcio Storico Fiorentino are held here every June). Lovely Renaissance palazzos surround the square: *Palazzo Cocchi-Serristori* (no. 1) by G. da Sangallo and *Palazzo dell'Antella* (on the right) with its long façade frescoed in 1620 by artists such as Passignano and Rosselli. You'll also find the family's coat-of-arms and a bust of Cosimo I. Further below you should also see the marble disk (1565) that marked the middle of the soccer field.

❷ Basilica of S. Croce

This church is considered the greatest expression of Florentine Gothic architecture. A. di Cambio began working on the church in 1294, but it was consecrated in 1442. In 1566, Vasari intervened drastically on the interior. In 1874, Baccani erected the bell tower. The basilica's neo-Gothic façade (1863) is the work of N. Matas (his tomb is located inside). On the sides of the church you can still see the original stone covering with its

characteristic drainpipes shaped like human and lion heads. On the steps that lead to the basilica you'll find **E. Pazzi**'s statue of *Dante* facing the square (1865).

The INTERIOR, in the form of an Egyptian cross, is divided into 3 naves by octagonal pillars. The central nave has a ceiling with trusses. Numerous chapels belonging to prominent families are found in the transept. The basilica has always been an important burial site for illustrious men. If you start at the counter-façade, you'll find the *Monument to Gino Capponi* (1884) and the *Monument to G.B. Niccolini* (1883). In the right nave: the *Tomb of Michelangelo* (1564) designed by **Vasari**, and in front, the *Madonna del Latte* (1478) by **A. Rossellino**. Next come the *Cenotaph of Dante Alighieri* (1829) and the neo-classical *Monument to Vittorio Alfieri* (1810) by **A. Canova**, with the statue of a *Weeping Italy*. Look for the splendid pulpit by **B. da Maiano** with tiles depicting *Scenes from the Life of St. Francis*. After ALTAR IV you'll reach the *Tomb of Niccolò Machiavelli* (1787) with the allegorical figure of *Diplomacy*. Also visit ALTAR V to see **Donatello**'s *Annunciation* (1433 ca.). Further ahead you'll come across **B. Rossellino**'s *Monument to Leonardo Bruni* (1445-1450), which served as a model for monumental tombs. Finally, the monuments to *Gioacchino Rossini* (1900) and *Ugo Foscolo* (1939) shouldn't be missed. ALTAR VI displays *Christ Entering Jerusalem* (1604) by **Cigoli**.

RIGHT TRANSEPT - The family chapels begin here. The CASTELLANI CHAPEL (the tertiary order would assemble here) was frescoed by **A. Gaddi** (1385) with the lives of saints. The BARONCELLI CHAPEL was decorated by **T. Gaddi** (1332-1338) with the *Life of the Virgin*. This best-known pupil of Giotto is also responsible for the stained glass window, whereas the polyptych with the *Coronation of the Virgin* was made by the master himself.

SACRISTY - If you pass through Michelozzo's doorway, you'll reach

B. da Maiano, Pulpit with Scenes from the Life of St. Francis

Pazzi Chapel

Cimabue, Crucifix

the room the Pazzi family commissioned. Here you'll find relics and anthem books. The room is frescoed by **S. Aretino** and T. Gaddi (*Crucifixion*). From here you'll reach the RINUCCINI CHAPEL, decorated by **G. da Milano** with *Stories from the Life of Magdalene* and *of the Virgin* (1363-1366). The original gate (1371) is still intact. Further behind, you can access the MEDICI CHAPEL, by Michelozzo, with its splendid altarpiece (*Madonna and Child*) in enameled terracotta by **A. della Robbia**.

Once you're back in the church, stop at the PERUZZI and BARDI CHAPELS, splendidly frescoed by Giotto between 1320 and 1325 with cycles dedicated to *St. John the Baptist* and *St. Francis*. In the Gothic, polygon-shaped MAIN CHAPEL, A. Gaddi's frescoes are dedicated to the story of the *Finding of the True Cross* (the church gets its name from this cycle). In the LEFT TRANSEPT, note the BARDI DI VERNIO CHAPEL frescoed by **M. di Banco** (1340 ca.) with *Stories of St. Sylvester*. Volterrano embellished (1664) the dome of the NICCOLINI CHAPEL, where two paintings by Allori and statues by P. Francavilla are also displayed. The Bardi family also owned another chapel closed off by a gate (1335) in which a wooden *Crucifix* sculpted by Donatello and a *ciborium* with two angels in gilded wood by Vasari can also be admired.

LEFT NAVE - The row of monuments begins again: you'll find the one dedicated to the musician *Luigi Cherubini* and to *Leon Battista Alberti*. ALTAR VI displays the *Pentecost* by **Vasari**. Next comes the the 15th-century tomb of *Carlo Marsuppini*, **D. da Settignano**'s masterpiece. ALTAR V displays the *Pietà* by **A. Bronzino**, and on the floor you'll find the tomb of *Lorenzo Ghiberti*. On ALTAR IV look for Vasari's *Doubting Thomas*. ALTAR II has the tomb of *Galileo Galilei* with a bust by **G.B. Foggini**.

Museum of the Opera di S. Croce (Piazza S. Croce, 16)
This museum is located in the former convent refectory. It was inaugurated in 1900 and contains interesting objects from the church and the convent. In the garden of the FIRST CLOISTER, look for the bronze statue by **H. Moore**, *Warrier*. To the right in the first room, you'll see a *Crucifix* by **Cimabue** (post-1272). This work was seriously damaged in the 1966 flood. In the background, you'll find the large fresco by **T. Gaddi** (1333) with the *Tree of the Cross, Sacred Stories*, and the *Last Supper*; on the side walls there are fragments from the church of the fresco by **A. Orcagna** with the *Triumph of Death, Last Judgement*, and *Hell*. To your left: the bronze statue of *St. Ludovic of Tolouse* (1424) by **Donatello**. If you pass through another lovely doorway by B. da Maiano, you'll reach the SECOND CLOISTER, created in 1453 in *pietra serena*. The S. Croce complex concludes with the PAZZI CHAPEL. Begun by Brunelleschi (1429-1430), the chapel was completed after 1470 due to financial problems on the part of the patron, Andrea de' Pazzi. The decorations on the wall present 12 tondos with figures of the *Apostles* in glazed ceramic by **L. della Robbia**.

❸ Palazzo Horne (Via dei Benci, 6)

This palazzo was built in the late 1400s by Cronaca. It belonged to the Corsi family (cloth merchants). In the early 1900s, it was purchased by the English collector H.P. Horne, Oscar Wilde's friend and great enthusiast of Florentine art. His goal was to re-create a genteel Renaissance residence.

"H.P. Horne" Foundation Museum
The collection comprises a vast assortment of objects (14th-16th cent.): paintings, sculptures, majolicas, glass objects, coins, documents, manuscripts, printed books. Here you'll find a lovely tondo with the *Holy Family* by **D. Beccafumi**, the *Allegory of Music* by **D. Dossi**, and a beautiful panel with *St. Stephen* by **Giotto**. Don't miss the small throne-shaped inlaid bed (15th cent.) and a sacristy chest in inlaid wood with geometrical motifs (Tuscan manufacture, 15th cent.). A fragment of a chest by **Filippino Lippi** is also impressive (15th cent.).

❹ Casa Buonarroti (Via Ghibellina, 70)

In his will, C. Buonarroti expressed his desire to open his house to the public; he wanted to give Florence his private collection, which had started with Michelangelo (he lived in this house between 1516 and 1525). The museum was opened in 1859, and the "Casa Buonarroti" Institute was established in 1965. Scholars can consult (by appointment) the well-stocked library and the collection of 200 drawings by Michelangelo, and visitors can admire the marble relief of

Giotto, St. Stephen, *Horne Museum*
Casa Buonarroti Museum: *Michelangelo*, Battle of the Centaurs
Madonna of the Stairs
Bargello Courtyard

the *Battle of the Centaurs* (before 1492) and the *Madonna of the Stairs* (1492), a bas-relief in marble created by using the *schiacciato* technique.

❺ Palazzo and Bargello National Museum (Via del Proconsolo, 4)
This building was first erected in 1255 and was initially used as the seat of power of the Captain of Florence. Considered the first permanent seat of the city's institutions, it was completed after some time. In later years, the Podestà and the Council of Justice took up residence here. In 1574, the Bargello, head of police, moved here. As a result, some rooms were converted into prisons and torture and execution areas (convicted persons were hanged from the windows). When the death penalty was abolished in 1782, Leopoldo II of Tuscany was the first (1857) to begin restoring the building; he moved the prisons elsewhere and opened the museum in 1865. Today, the Bargello is considered one of the most important museums in the world for its statue and weapon collections. A church dedicated to Magdalene is annexed to the building. In this church, you'll find the fresco of *Paradise* in which a *Portrait of Dante* by **Giotto** was discovered. The most important parts of the collection include works by Donatello and the donations made by the collectors L. Carrand and G. Franchetti. Courtyard: porticoed on 3 sides. At the center you'll see a well, which replaced the medieval gallows. The side with the staircase by Neri di Fioravanti (1345) is decorated with coats-of-arms in stone and glazed terracotta. Under the arcade you can admire sculptures by artists like Ammannati and Giambologna, as well as a *cannon* (also called *St. Paul's Cannon* for the saint's head sculpted on the bottom). The entrance on the east side of the courtyard will lead you to the Hall of 14th-Cen-

tury Works where you'll find sculptures such as the *Madonna with Child* by **T. di Camaino** and the *Three Acolytes* by **A. di Cambio**. Next is the Hall of Michelangelo where you'll see the unfinished *Pitti Tondo* (1504 ca.) that portrays Mary with Jesus and a young St. John the Baptist; then there's the *Bacchus* (1496-1497), *Brutus*, and the *David-Apollo* (1532). Works by Ammannati, Bandinelli, Cellini (look for his lovely *Bust of Cosimo I*, 1547, cast in bronze), and Giambologna (his spectacular *Flying Mercury*) are also displayed in this room. Upstairs in the loggia, with its 19th-century medieval-inspired frescoes, you'll see works from the 1500s including a series of animals (Giambologna's *Turkey* stands out). Next is the Hall of the General Council or Hall of Donatello. This room, dedicated to 15th-century Florentine sculptors, contains many works by **Donatello** including the famous *Bust-portrait of the Leader Niccolò da Uzzano* in multicolored terracotta, the *Marzocco*, a lion (symbol of the city), and the lovely *Atys-Amor*, a bronze cupid that tramples upon a serpent. The artist's most significant works follow: the bronze *David* (1440-1450) and *St. George*, from Orsanmichele and commissioned by the Guild of Armor and Sword Makers in 1416. **D. da Settignano** is credited with a *Young St. John the Baptist*, while the two tiles (one is by Ghiberti and the other is by Brunelleschi) for the Baptistery door competition depicting the *Sacrifice of Isaac* are also on display. Works by Michelozzo and L. della Robbia are also present.
In the Islamic Hall, objects in metal and ivory, majolicas, jewelry, weapons, and carpets (9th-15th cent.) can be admired.
The Carrand Hall gathers over 3,000 objects from Carrand's collection. A must-see: the *helmet plaque of Agilulf* (6th-7th cent.). There are also rooms dedicated to Andrea and Giovanni della Robbia.
Hall of Small Works in Bronze has a lovely bronze statue, *Hercules and Antaeus*, by **A. Pollaiolo** and the *Ganymede* by **Cellini**. But the

Michelangelo:
Bacchus;
Brutus;
Pitti Tondo
G. Vasari, Loggia del Pesce

room dedicated to ANDREA DEL VERROCCHIO is worth visiting for the striking bronze *David* (1465 ca.) commissioned by the Medici, the delicate *Lady with the Nosegay*, in marble, and the *Bust of Piero di Lorenzo de' Medici*, in terracotta. Here you'll also see works by other artists such as M. da Fiesole and A. Rossellino. The last room, dedicated to ARMORY, gathers arms of the Medici and from private collections.

❻ BADIA FIORENTINA (Via del Proconsolo)
A religious complex founded in 978 for the Benedictines by Willa, mother of Marquis Ugo di Toscana, who is buried here. It was enlarged in Cistercian Gothic style during the 1300s; in 1330, the bell tower was erected. Its interior was completely refurbished in the 1600s, and a new entrance was created on Via Dante Alighieri. The interior is shaped like a Greek cross, and is Baroque in style. Look especially for the *Madonna Appears to St. Bernard* by **Filippino Lippi** on the left wall, while in the left transept you'll find the marble and porphyry *Tomb of Marquis Ugo di Toscana* by **M. da Fiesole**. Through a door to the right of the presbytery you'll reach the evocative CLOISTER OF ORANGES: built by B. Rossellino (1432-1438) with two levels of Ionic columns, it was frescoed on the top part with *Episodes from the Life of St. Benedict*.

❼ CASA DI DANTE MUSEUM (Via S. Margherita, 1)
This small museum is located near to the house where Dante was born (today, a well-known restaurant can be found there). The building is a medieval-style reconstruction (early 1900s). Here you'll find documentation on Florence as it was during Dante's life and various editions of the *Divine Comedy*.

❽ PALAZZO NON FINITO (Via del Proconsolo, 12)
This palazzo was built for A. Strozzi in rustic ashlar-work in 1593 by Buontalenti who decorated a floor with images of bats and shells. Cigoli finished part of the work in 1604 when he built the courtyard. Today, this building is home to the NATIONAL MUSEUM OF ANTHROPOLOGY AND ETHNOLOGY, founded by P. Mantegazza in 1869. The material on display comes from the private collections of the Medici. It also contains finds of explorers and navigators such as T. Cook (1779) as well as objects from private collectors like P. Graziosi, who donated his collection to the museum in 1960. These objects are displayed in over 25 rooms, which are arranged according to continent. Visitors can take a veritable trip around the world!

❾ BORGO DEGLI ALBIZI
This is an interesting medieval street. It still has many 16th-century palazzos including (no. 26) *Palazzo Ramirez de Montalvo* with graffito work on the façade (based upon a design by Vasari). At no. 18 you'll find *Palazzo Altoviti*, also called Palazzo of the "Visacci" for the 15 marble busts depicting prominent Florentines.

Take some time to also see the PALAZZO AND CHURCH OF S. FIRENZE (Piazza S. Firenze) in Baroque style (1645) and the LOGGIA DEL GRANO (Via dei Neri-corner Via Castellani), dated 1619 and used as the grain market. It is decorated on the corner by a fountain and by the bust of Cosimo II on the central arch. There's also the LOGGIA DEL PESCE (Piazza dei Ciompi), which stands on the site where the famous Ciompi revolt took place (1378). Made by Vasari in 1567, it was intended for the Mercato Vecchio, and is decorated with multicolored terracotta tondos depicting sea creatures and the Medici coat-of-arms. The famous antiques flea market is also held nearby.

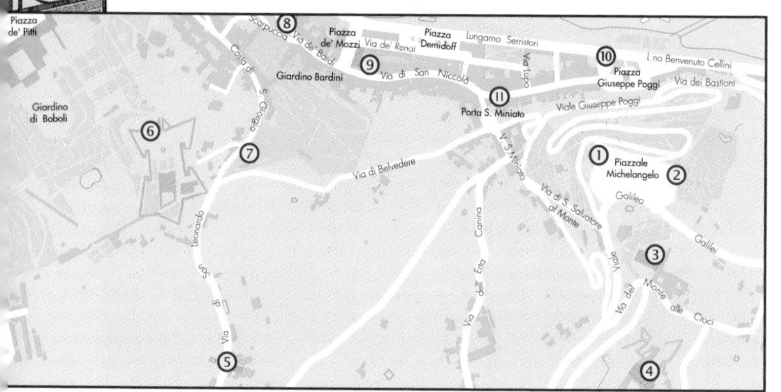

❶ **Piazzale Michelangelo** (*panoramic view)
If you head down Viale dei Colli, built by Poggi as a panoramic area and residential section for the well-to-do classes, you'll reach Piazzale Michelangelo, which will offer you a breathtaking view of the city. A monument to Michelangelo was placed here (1871); it's a copy of the celebrated *David* decorated at the base with statues (also copies) of the Medici tombs in S. Lorenzo. The loggia-café was also built by Poggi and is located on the opposite side of the square; it was originally supposed to be a museum that would house Michelangelo's works.

❷ **Iris Garden** (corner Viale dei Colli and Piazzale Michelangelo)
Opened in 1955, you can visit this splendid garden only during May. On your stroll you'll come across approximately 2,500 types of irises (since 1251 this flower has been the symbol of Florence).

Every year the Società Italiana dell'Iris holds a world-wide competition in which an award is given to the person who can obtain an iris with a rich vermilion color just like the one on the Medici coat-of-arms. No one, however, has truly been successful.

❸ Church of S. Salvatore al Monte

Take the stairs behind the loggia-café. Finished in 1504 by Cronaca, on the Mount of Crosses, this church has an unadorned façade. On the gable, observe the emblem of the Arte di Calimala (Guild of Imported Wool Refiners) that commissioned the church. The inside (1 nave with side chapels) was refurbished. Try to visit, in the left transept, the *Deposition of Christ* in glazed terracotta by **G. della Robbia**.

❹ Church of S. Miniato al Monte (*panoramic view)

This church rests upon pre-existing Christian constructions. In the 11th century, a Romanesque church dedicated to S. Miniato (he was martyred on this site, 4th cent.) was built here. Initially a Clunaic Benedictine basilica, it then passed to the Olivetan order. The bell tower was rebuilt by B. d'Agnolo in 1524, but it became famous during the 1530 siege of Florence because here Michelangelo set up the cannons that fired against the Imperial troops. It became, in 1552, a fortress. In fact, you can still see the entrance gates: the *de' Medici* gate and the *Soccorso* gate. In 1868, the staircase that connects the church to the Viale dei Colli was designed by Poggi.

The façade stands out for the contrast of white and green marble that alternate in geometric shapes on two levels: the top level corresponds to the central nave with a window that has a tympanum decorated with a 12th-century mosaic portraying *Christ En-*

Mosaicist, 13th cent., Christ Enthroned between Mary and St. Miniato, *detail*

Chapel of the Portuguese Cardinal

Crucifix Chapel

Florentine artists, Pulpit

throned between Mary and St. Miniato. On the spire observe the gilded copper eagle, the symbol of the Arte di Calimala (patrons of the church, 1401).

The INTERIOR, on 3 levels (crypt, main floor, raised presbytery), is divided into 3 naves by columns. The triumphal arch and the semi-circular apse bear innovative decorations, whereas the embellishment on the walls dates back to the 19th century. At the back of the central nave (the floor has marble inlays, 1207), you'll find the CRUCIFIX CHAPEL made by **Michelozzo** for Piero de' Medici (1448) with panels by **A. Gaddi** and coffers by the Della Robbia workshop in glazed terracotta on the barrel vault.

You'll arrive in the SACRISTY from the presbytery. It is square-shaped with a vault and large lunettes frescoed by **S. Aretino** with *Scenes from the Life of St. Benedict*. Go back into the presbytery and observe on the right an altar with a panel depicting the *Episodes of the Life of St. Miniato* (1320) by **J. del Casentino**. Observe the marble enclosure with transenna, the choir with inlaid wooden seats, the pulpit, and the main altar with a glazed terracotta *Crucifix* attributed to L. della Robbia.

The CRYPT (12th cent.) is the oldest part of the church and is covered with cross

vaults that rest upon 36 small columns made of different material (marble, *pietra serena*, terracotta) gilded in 1342. T. Gaddi is credited with the frescoes with a gold background on the vaults. CHAPEL OF THE PORTUGUESE CARDINAL - You'll arrive here from the left nave. It was built by Manetti in 1466. Its vault is decorated with 4 medallions in glazed terracotta by L. della Robbia that depict the *Cardinal Virtues*. The marble funerary monument was sculpted by the Rossellino brothers; frescoes adorn the walls and include the *Annunciation* (1466) by **A. Baldovinetti**. Next to the church you'll find the MONUMENTAL CEMETERY or cemetery of the "Holy Gates" begun in 1865 for the city's most prominent families. C. Lorenzini (Carlo Collodi) is also buried here.

❺ VIA DI S. LEONARDO

A picturesque road leading to the Forte Belvedere. Many artists lived in houses along this road, including the musician Tchaikovsky and the painter O. Rosai. You'll also find the CHURCH OF S. LEONARDO, an 11th-12th-century rural parish. It was refurbished in 1929 and contains a 13th-century marble *pulpit* from which Dante and Boccaccio spoke when it was located in the Church of S. Piero a Scheraggio before being demolished.

❻ FORTE BELVEDERE OR S. GIORGIO (open during exhibitions)

It was built in 1590 by Buontalenti for Ferdinando I. It was used as a defensive fort from attacks outside the city's walls, which can still be seen nearby. It overlooks and is connected to the Boboli Garden. Don't miss the breathtaking view of the city. (*PANORAMIC VIEW)
At the center you'll see the PALAZZINA DI BELVEDERE (1570), built upon a design attributed to Ammannati.

S. Giorgio Gate
Bardini Museum:
T. di Camaino, Charity
Donatello, Madonna dei Cordai

7 Costa S. Giorgio
Once you've passed the S. Giorgio Gate, which was once part of the second ring of walls, you'll come across a steep descent and one of the city's most characteristic streets, until you reach Via dei Bardi by passing along Costa Scarpuccia. At no. 17 of Costa S. Giorgio you'll see Galileo's house, decorated with his family's coats-of-arms and his bust on the façade.

8 Via de' Bardi
Once called the "Pitiglioso" section of town because greedy, stingy people lived here, it is divided into 2 parts: a more modern section towards Ponte Vecchio and the other towards S. Niccolò, closed off by lovely 14th-century palazzos that belonged to the most important merchant families. These include *Palazzo Capponi* (nos. 36-38), built for the banker Niccolò da Uzzano. The series of residences is interrupted by the Costa Scarpuccia *terre plein* support, which Cosimo I commissioned in 1547 after a disastrous landslide that destroyed various buildings. A plaque commemorates this tragic event. Right in front of the wall you'll find the Church of S. Lucia de' Magnoli or of the "Ruined," founded in 1078 and refurbished various times. Look for the panel with the *Madonna and Saints*, Florentine school (16th cent.), on the main altar. A tabernacle on the outside commemorates St. Francis who also stopped here.

9 Bardini Museum (Piazza dei Mozzi, 1)
This museum is currently being refurbished. It was established in 1881 in one of the 3 residences that belonged to the Bardini family (wealthy merchants). Stefano Bardini, a collector and antiques dealer, was an important figure in the late 1800s. In 1922, he left the Municipality of Flor-

ence his entire collection. The architecture of the residence itself is quite curious and includes decorative elements from various periods. Observe the altar dedicated to Augustus that depicts Dionysus (reused as a well-curb), a 12th-century capital with the *Nativity*, and the *Charity* marble sculpture by **T. da Camaino**. Don't miss the fireplaces and the Roman bath in porphyry as well as the Persian carpets and the rooms dedicated to armory. The works in terracotta are also interesting and include the *Madonna with Child*, attributed to **Donatello**, and the *Madonna dei Cordai* (by this same artist). You'll also find the CORSI GALLERY in this museum, donated to the Municipality of Florence in 1937; it gathers over 600 works from the 12th to 19th centuries. Near the museum you'll see the **BARDINI GARDENS** (Via dei Bardi, 1r), purchased in 1913 by S. Bardini. It is one of the most representative models of Italian-style gardens with a panoramic terrace overlooking the city. (*PANORAMIC VIEW)

10 S. NICCOLÒ GATE (Piazza G. Poggi)
The area created in 1866 by Poggi includes the centuries-old crenellated gate of S. Niccolò at the center. This gate was built in 1324 as a rampart along with the walls in order to defend this part of the city. It is the only original gate left in Florence. As you enter, you'll find a fresco with the *Madonna and Saints* (15th cent.). From here you can walk up the 2 flights of steps built by Poggi and reach Piazzale Michelangelo after passing lovely grottos and fountains.

11 S. MINIATO GATE
This 14th-century gate with a walkway on the wall that is supported by arches can be crossed as you go to the Church of S. Miniato a Monte, along Via del Monte alle Croci (also called the *Via Crucis*, built by the Franciscans).

11. OUTSIDE the WALLS

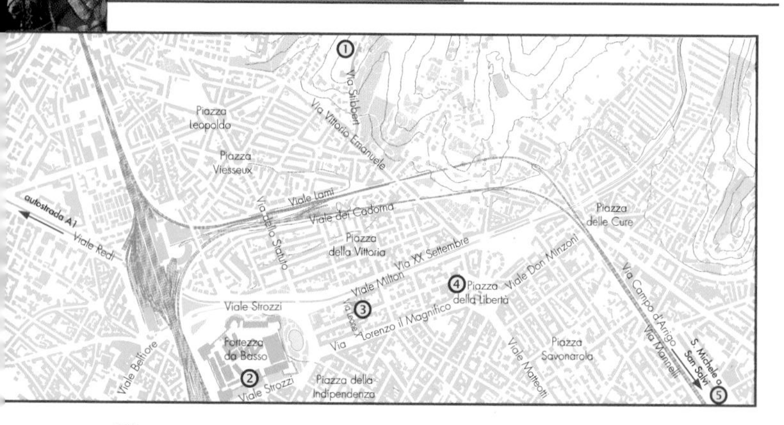

1 STIBBERT MUSEUM (Via Federico Stibbert, 26)
Nestled in a lovely park, this museum gathers one of the most important private collections in the world of centuries-old weapons and costumes. The collector was Frederick (or Federico) Stibbert, who was born in Florence (1838-1906); his father was English and his mother was Florentine. Heir to a vast patrimony, Federico stood out for his eclecticism: he was a painter, a member of the Florentine Accademia delle Belle Arti, a businessman, and a writer. Thanks to his incessant traveling, Stibbert was able to gather over 50,000 objects (from late 15th century to first Empire). His collection was then bequeathed to the British government who in turn donated it to Florence. In 1908, a foundation was established. Stibbert refurbished and enlarged his residence in order to house his collection and make it available to the public. Today, the museum is composed of over 60 rooms, including his family's liv-

ing quarters. Stibbert's intention was to recreate surroundings and furnishings suited to the collections on display. The most interesting objects are mentioned below, though keep in mind that their location in the museum may be subject to change.

ORIENTAL HALLS (6-8) - Gather Turkish and Persian weaponry and armor, *Turkmen suits of armor* (15th-19th cent.), and splendid *Indian weaponry and armor* (16th-18th cent.).

CAVALCADE HALL (9) with its Italian, German, and Ottoman *train of knights* (16th-17th cent.); in the STANZINO (small storage room, 11), you'll find the *German funerary corselet* of Giovanni of the Black Bands. As you're in the PASSAGEWAY (17), observe the *saber* of Gioacchino Murat, while in the MILITARY HALL (18), you'll find the *flag* of the second infantry regiment of the Kingdom of Italy.

COSTUME HALLS (38-41) - This collection is one of the most complete and richest in Europe and contains very rare pieces. Observe the male and female costumes as well as the liveries and accessories (16th-18th cent.). The FREDERICK STIBBERT ROOM (48) still has its original furniture, with mementos of his family and portraits. In the EMPIRE HALL (49), which belonged to

Japanese Rooms,

Funerary corselet of Giovanni of the Black Bands

Table with top in malachite

Napoleon's Grand Costume of Italy

A. del Sarto, Last Supper, *Cenacolo di A. del Sarto Museum*

his mother Giulia, you'll see the *ball gown* of a lady-in-waiting at the court of Elisa Baciocchi. In the EMPIRE LOGGETTA (50), you'll find the *Grand Costume of Italy* that Napoleon Bonaparte wore when he was crowned King of Italy in 1805.

JAPANESE ROOMS (55-58) - Observe the splendid *samurai group*, as well as the Japanese and Chinese weapons, helmets, and gear. Don't miss the painting collection, especially those by J. Suttermans, Bronzino, A. Allori, G.B. Tiepolo, and L. Giordano, and the collection of everyday objects such as clocks and watches, combs, cutlery, ceramics, fans, canes, and umbrellas.

This villa is surrounded by a wonderful English-style romantic park designed by Poggi. Here you'll find a pond with a small Egyptian-style temple and obelisk, a small Hellenic-style temple, and a greenhouse with rare exotic essences.

❷ FORTEZZA DA BASSO OR OF S. GIOVANNI

This fortress was built beginning in 1534 and was designed by A. da Sangallo the Younger for Alessandro de' Medici who feared internal strife more than outside invasion. Shaped like a pentagon, it takes up a vast area where today important events and exhibitions are held. Observe the keep, covered in *pietra forte*, and the octagonal guardhouse.

❸ RUSSIAN-ORTHODOX CHURCH (Via Leone X, 8)

It was built thanks especially to the donations of the Demidoff Russian princes during the early 1900s. It was designed by the architect M. Preobrazenskij and consecrated on November 8, 1903. It is square in shape and made of *pietra serena* with a base in *pietra forte*; its domes are made with Russian-style multicolored ceram-

ics and are topped by bronze crosses. The inside is adorned with stuccos, reliefs, icons, and paintings by G. Lolli. Czar Nicolas II donated the Carrara marble iconostasis.

❹ PIAZZA DELLA LIBERTÀ
Designed in the late 1800s by Poggi in Florentine Renaissance style. At the center you'll find the S. Gallo Gate (1285) with tabernacles decorated with lions and a 16th-century fresco in the lunette depicting the *Madonna, Child, and Saints*. On the north side you'll see the *Triumphal Arch of Francesco Stefano of Lorraine,* erected on the occasion of his entry into the city in 1739, topped by the *equestrian Monument of Francesco Stefano* by **G. B. Foggini**.

❺ COMPLEX OF **S. MICHELE A S. SALVI** (Via di S. Salvi, 16)
This religious complex is composed of the monastery of S. Salvi and the Church of S. Michele a S. Salvi, which dates back to 1048. The CENACOLO DI ANDREA DEL SARTO MUSEUM was set up in the former refectory in 1981. The room was frescoed by the artist in 1527 with the *Last Supper*; legend has it that this work was spared by the soldiers of Charles V because it was so extraordinarily beautiful. The museum also gathers other works by this artist including the *Annunciation* (1509 ca.) and the *Pietà* (1520 ca.). You'll also find paintings by R. del Garbo, Pontormo, and Vasari.

Try to visit the STATE ARCHIVE (Viale Giovane Italia, 6). It's one of the biggest in Europe and it also hosts temporary exhibitions. The ENGLISH OR PROTESTANT CEMETERY (Piazzale Donatello) was built in 1828 for the large English and Protestant community. E.B. Browning and G.P. Vieusseux are buried here.

12. AROUND FLORENCE

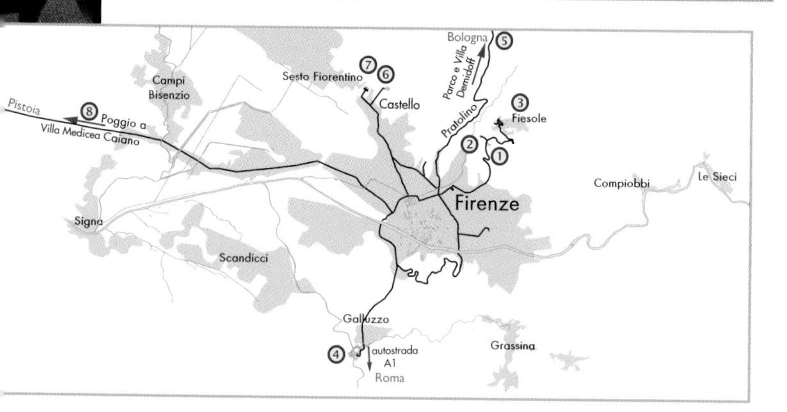

❶ On the Way to Fiesole – Convent of S. Domenico (Piazza S. Domenico)

As you head down the street, which leads to Fiesole, try to visit the church of S. Domenico, founded in 1406 by the Dominican friar Giovanni Baccini. St. Antonino, Bishop of Florence, and B. Angelico, who was the convent's prior, also lived here. The entrance is preceded by an elegant arcade erected in 1635 by Nigetti, who also built the bell tower. The interior consists of 1 nave with 6 chapels (15th-16th cent.) and is full of paintings. These include the triptych of the *Madonna with Child, Praying Angels, and Saints Barnabus, Dominic, Thomas of Aquinas, and Peter Martyr* by **Angelico** (the landscape and background architecture were redone by L. di Credi in 1501).

❷ Badia Fiesolana (Via Badia dei Roccettini)

The abbey dates to the early Middle Ages. Legend has it that this abbey was built over the site where St. Romulus was martyred. It acted as the cathedral of Fiesole and the residence of its bishops until 1028. In 1456, Cosimo the Elder had an apartment built inside which he used as a library and then as a meeting place for Florentine humanists. The unadorned façade of the Church is unfinished and incorporates the Romanesque one (12th cent.) in white and green marble. The interior (a single nave) has side chapels and dates back to the late 1400s. You'll find some lovely paintings (17th-18th cent.) on the altars.

❸ Fiesole

This town stands on the hill that overlooks the Arno and Mugnone Valleys. It once was an important center under the Etruscans (late 5th-6th cent. B.C.), the Romans (it became a Roman colony in 80 B.C. and was called *Faesulae*; it later became a *municipium* during the

1st cent. B.C.), and during the early Middle Ages. It underwent great decline at the time of the Langobards, and was subjugated by Florence in 1125. The Medici greatly enjoyed Fiesole, and starting in the 1700s it became a must-see for foreigners passing through Florence. In fact, here they built or resided in the numerous lovely villas (for example, W. Spence hosted in *Villa Medici* the English colony of Pre-Raphaelite painters and the artist A. Böcklin lived in Villa Bellagio in the late 1800s).

Fiesole:
Cathedral of S. Romolo
Following pages:
Roman Theater
Church of S. Francesco

Piazza Mino da Fiesole (*panoramic view)
The ancient Roman forum was once located below this square. To the left you'll find the grandiose *Seminary* (1637) and the *Bishop's Palazzo* (erected in the 11th century with a façade dating to 1675). On the north side you'll see the Duomo. The east side is closed off by the 14th-century Palazzo Pretorio (Town Hall is located here today), with its porticos and loggia that bears the coats-of-arms of the Podestà (1520-1808). Nearby you'll find the Church of S. Maria Primerana (mentioned in documents as early as 966), refurbished in the late 1500s in the mannerist style with graffito decorations. It was completed in 1801 by its portico.

CATHEDRAL OF **S. ROMOLO**

Built in the 11th century and enlarged during the 13th century, it was radically refurbished in the 1800s. Its crenellated bell tower dates back to the 13th century. The INTERIOR is composed of 3 naves supported by stone columns. It has a raised apse above the crypt that lies below. Here you'll find many important statues like *St. Romulus* (1521) in multicolored terracotta by G. della Robbia on the COUNTER-FAÇADE; in the presbytery on the right, you'll see the SALUTATI CHAPEL with frescoes by C. Rosselli and the *Tomb of Bishop Leonardo Salutati* by **M. da Fiesole**. Have a look at the MAIN ALTAR and the polyptych *Madonna with Child and Saints* by **B. di Lorenzo**. In the SACRISTY (18th cent.), centuries-old ecclesiastical objects are displayed. In the 13th-century CRYPT, a granite *Baptismal Font* (1569) by **F. del Tadda** is located on the right.

BANDINI MUSEUM (Via G. Duprè, 1, currently being refurbished)

Opened to the public in 1913, this museum houses the canon Angelo Maria Bandini's collection, which was bequeathed to the Bishop and the Chapter of Fiesole in 1803. This collection is mostly made up of Florentine paintings and sculptures (1200s-1400s) as well as other objects and sculptures of later centuries, including many pieces by the Della Robbia workshop. Artists include T. Gaddi, B. Daddi, N. and J. di Cione, J. del Sellaio, L. Monaco.

ARCHEOLOGICAL AREA (Via Marini, 1) (*PANORAMIC VIEW)

This area includes a THEATER, which is still used during the summer, built at the time of Augustus; it can seat 3,000 people and is 34 meters in diameter. Situated on the side of the hill, the theater is divided into 4 sectors by 3 flights of steps. The stage in front of the orchestra is supported by a small wall. To the side you can see the niche that

once held the puller used to raise and lower the curtain. The BATHS, which also date back to the time of Augustus, are near the theater, but are marked off by the Etruscan walls. The ROMAN TEMPLE, rebuilt after a fire in the 1st century B.C., has a tympanum adorned with terracotta figures and a staircase with 7 steps. Observe the ruins of the 5 columns that held up the portico. The ETRUSCAN TEMPLE, built during the 3rd century B.C., was dedicated to a divinity that brought health and wellbeing; the flight of steps and the remains of the roof decorations (now at the Civic Museum) are still visible.
CIVIC MUSEUM - Founded in 1873, it displays objects and finds from the Etruscan, Roman, and Medieval periods found in and around Fiesole. Among the most interesting works: cinerary urns, found in Etruscan tombs (2nd-3rd cent. B.C.) from the nearby Via del Bargellino, bronze statuettes portraying animals and humans, glass wine chalices used by the Langobards, ceramics. Don't miss the stele in *pietra serena* with scenes of a banquet, dancing, and hunting (first-half, 5th cent. B.C.). Since 1985 the A. Costantini Collection, donated to the Municipality of Fiesole, has been housed in the ANTIQUARIUM COSTANTINI (Via Portigiani, 9). It comprises about 170 objects in ceramic from Attica, Etruruia, and Magna Graecia.

PRIMO CONTI FOUNDATION (Via G. Duprè, 18)
In the 16th-century *Villa le Coste*, you'll find the archive and collection of the painter P. Conti who passed away in 1988. He is buried in the chapel (located in the garden), decorated with paintings from the late 1600s.

HILL OF ST. FRANCIS (Via di S. Francesco)
If you travel up the steep hill, you'll reach the *Garden of Remembrance*, which offers a breathtaking view of Florence. (*PANORAMIC

VIEW) Continue along and you'll arrive at the hill that in ancient times was the Etruscan-Roman acropolis. Here you'll see a religious complex composed of the Basilica of S. Alessandro, the Church of S. Francesco, and the Church of S. Cecilia.
The most interesting of the three is the CHURCH OF S. FRANCESCO. Built in the 1300s for the Florentine women hermits, it passed to the Franciscans later that century. It was refurbished in the early 1900s, though it still maintains its 15th-century façade and a portion of its left side. The INTERIOR (a single nave) contains many works including the *Annunciation* by R. del Garbo on ALTAR II to the left. In the CHAPEL OF S. ANTONIO, there's the *Manger Scene* in terracotta by the Della Robbia workshop. From the 15th-century cloister, near the sacristy, you'll reach the MISSIONARY MUSEUM OF ETHNOGRAPHY, which contains Etruscan and Chinese objects as well as an Egyptian mummy.

❹ GALLUZZO CHARTERHOUSE (entrance Buca di Certosa, 2)
Along the Via Senese, you'll find the Charterhouse that dominates, from Mount Acuto (110 meters), the Val d'Ema. This monastery was founded in 1342 by will of N. Acciaioli; it was later enlarged and embellished thanks to the bequests of many noble Florentine families. In 1810, following French suppression, the monastery also possessed a rich library (now completely lost) and over 500 works of art. Among the works currently housed in the PICTURE GALLERY: 5 large lunettes with *Episodes of the Passion* (1525) by **Pontormo**. The CHURCH OF S. LORENZO and the CHURCH OF MONKS (both dating to the 14th cent.) are also part of the complex, and inside you'll find works by Florentine and Tuscan artists (1500s-1600s). Don't miss the splendid inlaid walnut stalls (late 16th cent.) in the second church.
MAIN CLOISTER - Built in the early 16th century, its architecture is Renaissance in style. In the arch pendentives, there are 66 busts in glazed terracotta (apostles, saints, evangelists, and figures from the Old Testament) from the G. della Robbia workshop. On three sides of the cloister you'll see various monk cells, each of which also had a vegetable patch.

❺ VILLA DEMIDOFF-PRATOLINO AND PARK (Via Bolognese, seasonal opening)
If you continue along highway 65 (direction: Bologna), you'll reach this immense park that today belongs to the Province of Florence. The land was purchased in 1568 by Francesco I de' Medici who asked Buonatalenti to build a villa and a garden with grottoes, fountains, and statues. Over the following years, it became one of the most important sites for cultural events in Florence, and in 1683 concerts by Scarlatti and Händel were held here. The villa was demolished in

1824 under the Lorraines, but the immense park was spared. In 1872, the Savoy family sold the property to the Demidoffs, who then erected a new villa. The most important work is the *Apennine* fountain (1589) by **Giambologna**, with its splendid grottos. Nearby you'll also see a stone dragon by G. B. Foggini. Don't miss *Cupid's Grotto* (1577) and the CHAPEL by Buontalenti with its small dome and portico with plaques that commemorate the Demidoff family.

Giambologna, Apennine, *Villa Demidoff Park*

If you can, try to stop by the Medici villas outside Florence. ❻ VILLA PETRAIA (Via della Petraia, 40) and ❼ VILLA DI CASTELLO (Via di Castello, 47) were purchased by the Medici during the 16th century; here Tribolo created the marvelous three-level gardens, of which the Italian-style ones are considered the most beautiful in Europe. The splendid ❽ VILLA MEDICI OF POGGIO A CAIANO (Piazza de' Medici, 12, Poggio a Caiano), which still maintains its original medieval fortress structure surrounded by a ring of walls with small towers at the corners, is famous for having been Lorenzo the Magnificent's preferred villa. In fact, he had it refurbished in the classical style with a Greek temple-shaped entrance. Try to visit the museum located inside the villa.

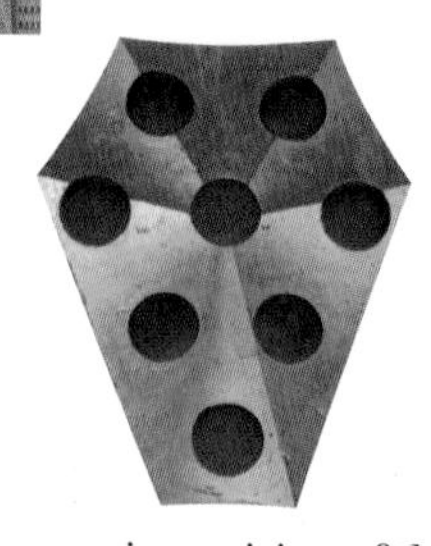

The Medici and Florence—two names that are inextricably linked to each other. Beginning in the Middle Ages, but more specifically between the Renaissance and the 18th century, the personality, culture, and sensibility of the Medici sovereigns united itself to the city's vitality, nurtured by the people who lived here: artists, poets, men of letters as well as artisans and workers who were able to interpret a unique vision of the world that was oftentimes innovative and visionary. They are responsible for the breathtaking art we all admire today, and have created one of the world's greatest city-museums.

The first Medici who played an important role in the city's history was **Giovanni d'Averardo**, known as **"di Bicci"** (Florence ? 1360–1429). He established the most powerful dynasty in Florence's history and was able to lay the foundations for a Republic that paid attention to the needs of the middle and lower classes.
In 1413, Giovanni became the trustee of anti-Pope John XXIII. In this role, he was able to pave the way to his family's economic rise and to co-participate in the business dealings of the Curia. After having opened various money exchange branches in Venice, Rome, and Naples, in 1421 he was elected Gonfalonier of Florence, thereby giving life to a policy that was aimed at obtaining almost absolute power by way of consent from the middle and lower classes. A promoter of the arts, Giovanni, in 1421, entrusted Brunelleschi with building "the Sacristy and a chapel" inside the Church of S. Lorenzo by sponsoring a part of the transept and the longitudinal section connected to the ancient basilica. In this way, Giovanni began the radical transformation of what would become the private church of the Medici. This project would be completed by his heirs.

Giovanni's successor was **Cosimo**, his son, known as **the Elder** or "Pater Patriae" (Florence 1389–1464). Cosimo was very intelligent and had a striking personality, which he expressed in his business dealings and intellectual interests, especially in his appreciation of philosophy. An opponent of Florentine aristocracy, he was forced into exile from 1432 to 1434, but when he returned he led the Medici family to complete dominion of the city and the entire region of Tuscany. A promoter of the *Platonic Academy* and a collector of the first core of codices that would later constitute the *Medici-Laurentian Library*, Cosimo was an art lover as well. The friend of B. Angelico and P. Uccello, he was particularly fascinated with Donatello. In fact, he commissioned this artist with the stucco decorations and the bronze doors in the Old Sacristy and the (unfinished) bronze pulpits in S. Lorenzo, in addition to the statues of *David* and *Judith and Holofernes*. Michelozzo was Cosimo's preferred architect. He was asked to build Palazzo Medici on Via Larga, the Badia Fiesolana, the convent of S. Marco, the Novitiate Chapel in S. Croce, and the Church of the Annunziata.

Piero the Gouty (Florence 1416–1469) came to power at the age of 48 and, despite some initial difficulties, he was able, starting in 1466, to win back support for his short-lived reign, which lasted a mere five years. He had been sent abroad by his father to follow the family business at the most important courts of the age. The King of France granted him the right to place the *fleur-de-lys* upon his family's coat-of-arms. A good scholar of Latin, Piero loved the decorative arts, which he enthusiastically collected. Some of his favorite painters included D. Veneziano and B. Gozzoli, who was commissioned with the chapel of the Palazzo Medici. He admired L. della Robbia for the preciousness of his majolicas and the inventiveness with which he used marble and glazed terracotta. He also praised Michelozzo, who was asked to build the small temple in SS. Annunziata and the Crucifix Chapel in S. Miniato al Monte.

Under **Lorenzo**, known by his contemporaries as **the Magnificent** (Florence 1449–1492), Florence flourished and became, thanks to extraordinary patronage, the "new Athens." Despite the conspiracy on the part of his enemies (especially Luca Pitti) who tried to eliminate the dynasty and the difficult political crisis when Papal and Neapolitan troops (1479) arrived in the city, Lorenzo was able to react with great skill. His talent for mediating allowed him to quickly form an alliance with the King of Naples, Ferrante, and to put an end to this turbulent situation. Lorenzo attended the *Platonic Academy* and was a refined man of letters. He wrote works of all kinds in vulgate and was a great patron of the arts. He carried on the patronage of his predecessors and collaborated with many artists. Some of his most favorite artists included A. del Verrocchio (Leonardo da Vinci and Perugino trained in his workshop that created objects in gold, sculptures, and paintings), who made the *Baptism of Christ*, the statue *David* (for the villa of Careggi, today housed in the Bargello Museum), and the innovative *Putto with Dolphin*, presently found in Palazzo Vecchio. He also admired Filippino Lippi, whose reputation among his contemporaries was boosted thanks to Lorenzo. G. da Sangallo was the Magnificent's preferred architect and interpreter of the aristocratic and neo-platonic ideals in vogue in Florence during those years. This architect was able to translate the basic principles of the philosophy of the age into the ideal of perfect forms. This is especially evident in the works commissioned by Lorenzo: the Church of S. Maria delle Carceri in Prato, the sacristy of S. Spirito, and the Villa di Poggio a Caiano.

Piero, known as **the Unfortunate** (Florence 1472?–Gaeta 1503), Lorenzo's son, reigned for just two years (1492–1494). Even though he, too, was educated and erudite, Piero was nothing in comparison to his father. In fact, he committed a series of grave political mistakes. He was forced to leave Florence with his brothers Giovanni, future Pope Leo X, and Giuliano. After the Medici fled from the city, the family's immense patrimony, made up of art objects, furnishings, and priceless manuscripts, was looted by the enraged masses. This brought about the dispersion of a veritable treasure-trove, collected during the golden age of Florence's art and culture.
The Medici returned to Florence in 1512.

Giuliano (Florence 1479–1516), elected **Duke of Nemours** by the King of France, ruled for one year (until 1513). However, he was praised and admired for his skill as a mediator and for his honesty. In 1513, he moved to Rome with the title Gonfalonier of the Papal Army—a position he was given by his brother Giovanni who had been elected Pope Leo X (Florence 1475-Rome 1521).
Giuliano was buried in the New Sacristy of S. Lorenzo. His sepulchral effigy was made by Michelangelo.

Lorenzo Duke of Urbino (Florence 1492–1519), son of Piero the Unfortunate, was initially loyal to the political policies of the Medici pope, Leo X (in fact, this pope granted Lorenzo many privileges). However, he soon distanced himself, thereby revealing his insatiable ambitiousness.

The illegitimate son of Giulio de' Medici (Pope Clement VII, Florence 1478–Rome 1534), **Alessandro** (Florence 1511–1537) acted as the city's first duke. Shrewd and revengeful, he became a tyrant. He married Margherita, the daughter of Emperor Charles V, but was assassinated a few months later by his cousin Lorenzino, nicknamed "Lorenzaccio."

After Alessandro's untimely death, the responsibility of ruling the city fell into the hands of the very young **Cosimo** I (Florence 1519–1574). The son of Giovanni of the Black Bands, he chose to ally himself with the Emperor. In 1539, he wed Eleanor, the daughter of the Viceroy of Naples, Pedro of Toledo. Together with his wife, he left his palace on Via Larga and moved to Palazzo della Signoria. During his reign, Cosimo was able to consolidate the Duchy's political and economic policies. He managed to almost double the size of his domain when he acquired Siena. He also created a war fleet, established the Ordine Militare di S. Stefano, opened silver mines in Pietrasanta and marble quarries in Carrara, was allowed to process alum in Piombino, and set up a strategic garrison in Portoferraio.

Cosimo reaped the rewards of his actions in 1569 when Pope Pious V gave him the title of Grand Duke. But all these accomplishments were outshined by the saddest defeat of all: in 1562, his children Giovanni and Garzia died from a terrible fever. His beloved wife Eleanor followed shortly after.

Deprived of his wife who had been an intelligent and loyal advisor that helped him with her riches and supported him politically by means of her father's precious interventions with the pope, in 1564 Cosimo decided to withdraw from public life. He appointed his son Francesco as successor.

Cosimo was also an exceptional patron of the arts. In 1547, he commissioned the Loggia of the Mercato Nuovo and in 1548, he

decided to open the Medici-Laurentian Library (Giorgio Vasari was asked to complete the work Michelangelo had started) to the public. In 1554, Cellini's *Perseus* was placed under the Loggia della Signoria. In 1555, he entrusted G. Vasari with the task of transforming Palazzo della Signoria into a residence fit for a prince. In 1560, Vasari was asked to build the Uffizi and its Corridor (today known as Vasari's Corridor) that united Palazzo Vecchio with Palazzo Pitti, which was purchased by Eleanor in 1549 and enlarged by B. Ammannati. In 1563, Cosimo founded the Accademia delle Arti e del Disegno, which is the first art academy in Europe.
Moreover, this Grand Duke changed Tuscany from an architectural point of view as he commissioned fortresses and fortified structures throughout the entire territory to the most prominent military architects of the age. His last public commission was the cycle of paintings for the dome in the Duomo. Vasari was entrusted with this task in 1574, but neither Cosimo nor the artist was able to see the finished dome since both died that very same year.

Cosimo's son, **Francesco** I (Florence 1541–1587) acted as regent until his father died, and governed from 1574 to 1587. Bashful and reticent, he repressed a conspiracy against himself on the part of the main families in Florence. As a result, hostilities increased. Francesco tried to continue with Cosimo's line of action, maintaining good relationships with Spain and the Empire. However, he always preferred his great passions to politics: science and alchemy. In fact, he conducted many studies in pharmacology and physics.
Francesco's name is inextricably tied to that of Bianca Cappello, an extraordinarily beautiful Venetian woman. The Grand Duke loved her so much that he publicly boasted of their relationship while he was still married to Arch Duchess Giovanna of Austria. In 1578, two months after Giovanna died, Bianca finally became his legitimate wife and Grand Duchess of Tuscany. Francesco and Bianca remained together until they passed away. In fact, Francesco died a few short hours before Bianca on October 21, 1587 in their villa at Poggio a Caiano.
His so-called *Studiolo* is famous for its artistic quality and originality. Francesco wanted it to be located near the Salone dei Cinquecento in Palazzo Vecchio. In order to build this small study, inspired by the bonds between natural elements and human artifice according to the fundamental principles of alchemy, the Grand Duke called upon artists

such as Vasari, Bronzino, Ammannati, and Giambologna who created a veritable "Wunderkammer," or room of wonders, embellished with splendid painted panels behind which small cabinets and treasure-troves hid rare and curious objects. Moreover, Francesco was very passionate about rock crystal, semi-precious stones, porcelain, and ceramic, which he even experimented with at times. His preferred artist was the eclectic Buontalenti, superintendent of public works and expert in all sorts of arts. He was asked to make various kinds of objects, including bowls and vases in semi-precious stones, and stage designs. He would even plan festivities and firework shows. In fact, Buontalenti was so famous for this that he was nicknamed "Bernardo delle girandole" ("Pinwheel Bernardo"). But this Grand Duke's intellectual masterpiece was the Uffizi, where he gathered the Medici collections and the octagonal Tribune designed by Buontalenti. Francesco also contributed to increasing the number of Medici villas. Special mention must be made of Villa Pratolino, built by Buontlaneti and nestled in an immense park with grottos, fountains, and machines, including the towering giant *Apennine* by Giambologna.

By will of his father Cosimo, Pope Pious v elected him cardinal at the age of 14. But in 1587, when Francesco died, his brother **Ferdinando** I (Florence 1549–1609) gave up the title of cardinal in order to become Grand Duke. Ferdinando was a peaceful sovereign who was able to re-establish serenity and win back the trust of his contemporaries. Through a series of marriages, especially the one to Christina of Lorraine, he attempted to consolidate the power of the Medici family with some of the most important families in Europe. He overturned former political alliances and strengthened ties with France while distancing himself from Spain. In 1588, Ferdinando founded the Galleria dei Lavori, later called the Opificio delle Pietre Dure, and commissioned the Forte Belvedere as well as the Villa Ambrogiana in Montelupo and the Villa of Artimino. He asked Giambologna to make the equestrian monument dedicated to Cosimo I, placed in Piazza della Signoria in 1594, and P. Tacca to execute a monument for himself for Piazza SS. Annunziata.

Cosimo II (Florence 1590–1621) definitively put an end to the Medici family's banking activities. He appointed Galileo Galilei Professor of Mathematics in Florence. A learned and generous man, he was constantly ill.

Cosimo died when he was just 31. He promoted the enlargement of Palazzo Pitti (entrusted to G. Parigi in 1618), whereas he asked his wife Maria Maddalena of Austria to rebuild Villa di Poggio Imperiale (it was called this way because of its Hapsburg origins). The Grand Duke introduced Florence to new types of painting that were in vogue in Europe during those years. He invited J. Callot and F. Napolitano to the city, and in 1620, he appointed J. Suttermans as the portraitist of the Medici. Before his untimely death, Cosimo II left a detailed will with precise instructions: he wished to entrust the regency to the Grand Duchesses, Christina of Lorraine and Maria Maddalena of Austria, respectively grandmother and mother of his son, who was the legitimate heir although still a minor. Hard times were in store for Florence: a sharp drop in trade, the Black Death that struck the city between 1630 and 1633, the effects of the 8 years of regency during which these two women wasted enormous amounts of public money.

When **Ferdinando** II (Florence 1610–1670) came into power, he was forced to deal with serious economic and health problems on the part of Florence's inhabitants. In the attempt to unite the Duchy of Urbino and the Grand Duchy of Tuscany, it was decided that Ferdinando would marry his cousin Vittoria della Rovere. But, despite the marriage, the union of these two states never actually took place because Pope Urban VIII was contrary.

A learned man who loved the arts, Ferdinando II contributed in a fundamental way to revitalizing the city's intellectual life. He promoted the Accademia del Disegno, the Accademia della Crusca, the Accademia degli Alterati, the Accademia degli Immobili, and the Accademia degli Infocati. In 1637, he refurbished the façade of the Church of Ognissanti and in 1640, he placed the equestrian monument to Ferdinando I in Piazza SS. Annunziata. He even commissioned G. da San Giovanni, F. Furini, C. Bravo, and O. Tannini with the decorations for the great hall of the summer apartments in Palazzo Pitti. His taste for the Roman Baroque art of P. da Cortona was rather innovative; in fact, this artist frescoed the winter apartments in Palazzo Pitti. Ferdinando received many masterpieces from his wife Vittoria's dowry. Today, these can be found in Florence's museums. They include the *Portrait of the Dukes of Urbino* by Piero della Francesca, the *Venus of Urbino* by Titian, and various works by Raphael. He also collected clocks, chests, games, and objects made with semiprecious stones that he systematically chose with impeccable taste.

Grand Duke **Cosimo** III (Florence 1642–1723) was, unlike his predecessors, a mediocre man who contributed (also because of his rather long reign, 1670–1723) to Florence's decline. Weak and a religious zealot, he installed a reign of terror during which Jews were persecuted (this was the only instance during the course of the entire Medici dynasty). Cosimo's only merit was that of having tried to resolve the Medici family's dynastic difficulties. Since his male sons had no children, he decided to destine the Grand Duchy to his daughter Maria Luisa. In this way, he aimed to ensure the autonomy of Tuscany. Nonetheless, it was only due to the decision reached by the great powers in Vienna in 1734 that Tuscany eventually passed into the hands of the Lorraine family. In the field of culture and the arts, Cosimo continued building the Chapel of Princes in S. Lorenzo, and his love for nature led him to collect still lifes. Among his most favorite artists: C. Dolci and the sculptor G. Zumbo, who created rather original, oftentimes macabre, works in wax. Ferdinando, Cosimo's first-born son who died at a young age in 1713, was a great admirer of art and enthusiast of Venetian painting. He purchased many works including the *Madonna del Baldacchino* by Raphael, the *Madonna delle Arpie* by A. del Sarto, and the *Madonna dal collo lungo* by Parmigianino.

Cosimo was succeeded by his son **Gian Gastone** (Florence 1671–1737). He is remembered as being rather lax in his habits and somewhat of a misanthrope. Nonetheless, he tried to remedy the persecutory laws his father had imposed. He commissioned a monument to Galileo that was then placed inside S. Croce.

Cosimo III's daughter, **Anna Maria Luisa** (Florence 1667–1743), was the last Medici to rule Tuscany. By marrying Giovanni Guglielmo, she was given the title of Electress Palatine. Anna was an intelligent and enlightened sovereign who carried out a generous act just a few years before she died in 1737: she donated the immense artistic patrimony the Medici had collected over the centuries to the Grand Duchy of Tuscany. Thanks also to her, the Medici have won an important place in history.

HANDY INFORMATION

MILITARY CORPS: tel. 112 · EMERGENCY HEALTH ASSISTANCE: tel. 118

STATE POLICE: tel. 113 · FIRE-FIGHTERS: tel. 115

"AMERIGO VESPUCCI" AIRPORT (Via del Termine, 11): tel. 055.30615 • 055.3061300

ATAF (urban transportation) information: Box Ataf in Piazza Stazione - "ProntoAtaf" tel. 800.424500, www.ataf.net. It's possible to take a quick city tour by riding the typical red double-decker of FIRENZE CITY SIGHTSEEING, with a choice of different itineraries.

PARKING IN FLORENCE: tel. 055.2720131, www.firenzeparcheggi.it

TAXIS: tel. 055.4242 • 055.4390

TRENITALIA - TRAIN ASSISTANCE (Piazza della Stazione, 1): tel. 055.219656

CENTRAL POST OFFICE (Via Pellicceria, 3): tel. 055.218156, (hours: Mon-Fri 8:30 am-7 pm, Sat 8:30 am-12:30 pm)

MUNICIPALITY OF FLORENCE OFFICIAL WEB SITE: www.comune.firenze.it

FLORENCE TOURIST PROMOTION (APT) - Province of Florence - Municipality of Florence (Via Cavour, 1r): tel. 055.290832-3, www.firenzeturismo.it

TOURIST INFORMATION OFFICE (Piazza della Stazione, 4): tel. 055.212245.

ITA CONSORTIUM TOURIST AND HOTEL INFORMATION (inside the S. Maria Novella Train Station): tel. 055.282893

"FIRENZE MUSEI" - information and booking (State Museums): tel. 055.294883, www.firenzemusei.it

WEEKLY MARKET: Parco delle Cascine (Viale degli Olmi) Tuesday mornings (hours: 8 am-1 pm). Offers food, flowers, household items, fabrics, clothing. Stretches for 3 km down a tree-lined avenue.

TYPICAL FLORENTINE FOOD includes: chicken liver *crostini*, dark cabbage *crostoni*, *finocchiona* (a kind of seasoned pork salami), *sbriciolona* (softer version of the finocchiona), large egg noodle pasta with

boar or hare sauce, *ribollita* (vegetable and bread soup), *pappa al pomodoro* (soft bread and tomato salad), *acquacotta* (bread and vegetable broth), *panzanella* (soft bread and vegetable salad), steaks, stewed peppered beef, tripe, *lampredotto* (lean, hand-sliced tripe), dried salt-cured cod, *fagioli all'uccelletto* (beans with seasoned tomato sauce). Desserts include: *torta della nonna* (shortbread cake with cream and pine nuts), rice pudding, semolino cake, *cantuccini* with *Vin Santo*, *schiacciata* (thin sponge cake) and *cenci* (fried thin pastry dough) during Carnival, *pan di ramerino* (bread with rosemary) and *quaresimali* (chocolate alphabet-shaped cookies) during Easter, *schiacciata con l'uva* (thin sponge cake with raisons) and *castagnaccio* (chestnut flour cake) in the fall. The typical bread is insipid, whereas salty flat breads are excellent for a light snack. There is a vast selection of restaurants, but we recommend: *Buca Lapi* (Via del Trebbio, 1r) and *Trattoria Da Ginone* (Via dei Serragli, 35r), both run by local families. For sinful treats(!) try: traditional truffled sandwiches at *Procacci* (Via Tornabuoni, 64r), warm donuts (since 1943) at *Cucciolo* (Via del Corso, 25r), a great sandwich at *Fratellini* (Via de' Cimatori, 38r), ice cream at *Perché no?* (Via dei Tavolini, 19r), and chocolate at *Hemingway* (Piazza Piattellina, 9r).

PUBLIC EVENTS:
January 6 - *Ride of the Magi*: traditional historical parade through the city's main streets with participants in Renaissance costumes.
Easter Sunday - *Scoppio del Carro* (Piazza Duomo): after mass in the Duomo, a mechanical "small dove" is burned as it flies about. It causes the majestic cart placed outside the cathedral and loaded with fireworks to explode. If all goes as planned, the coming year will be a good one!
June 24 - *Calcio Storico Fiorentino* match (Piazza S. Croce): popular medieval soccer game between the 4 Florentine neighborhoods, preceded by a historical parade with 530 participants in period costumes.
June 24 - *Fòchi di S. Giovanni* (Piazzale Michelangelo): feast of Florence's patron saint with an evening firework show.

SHOPPING IN FLORENCE: typically Florentine products and traditions include embroidery (*TAF* is quite famous, Via Por S. Maria, 22r), paper (*Giannini*, Piazza Pitti, 37r), silver (*Brandimarte*, Via L. Ariosto, 11/C-R), leather (*Parri's*, Via Guicciardini, 18r), perfume (*Officina Profumo-Farmaceutica di Santa Maria Novella*, Via della Scala, 16), and silk (*Antico setificio fiorentino*, Via Bartolini, 4).
If you wish to purchase some good wine, the best retailers are: *Enoteca Bonatti* (Via V. Gioberti, 66r) and *Zanobini* (Via S. Antonino, 47r).

OUR FOUR-LEGGED FRIENDS: pet-friendly area located in the park of Villa il Boschetto (Via di Soffiano, 11) and in Parco delle Cascine (Viale degli Olmi).
Please remember that all pet waste must be disposed. Violators will be fined.

Index of Sights

printed in May 2009
by Genesi, Città di Castello
for
s i l l a b e